How to
Succeed
at being
yourself

How to
Succeed
at being
yourself

Finding the Confidence
to Fulfill Your Destiny

JOYCE MEYER

Faith
Words

NEW YORK   BOSTON   NASHVILLE

FaithWords Edition
Copyright © 1999 by Joyce Meyer
Life In The Word, Inc.
P. O. Box 655
Fenton, Missouri 63026

FaithWords
Hachette Book Group USA
237 Park Avenue, New York, NY 10017
Visit our Web site at www.faithwords.com.

Printed in the United States of America

First FaithWords Edition: October 2002
10 9 8 7

FaithWords is a division of Hachette Book Group USA, Inc.
The FaithWords name and logo are trademarks of Hachette Book Goup USA, Inc.

ISBN 978-0-446-53204-4
LCCN: 2002110832

CONTENTS

INTRODUCTION

INTRODUCTION

This book is about knowing yourself, accepting yourself and fulfilling your God-ordained destiny.

During my years in ministering to others, I have discovered that most people really

May Christ through your faith [actually] dwell (settle down, abide, make His permanent home) in your hearts! May you be rooted deep in love and founded securely on love.
EPHESIANS 3:17

don't like themselves. This is a very big problem, much bigger than one might think initially.

If we don't get along with ourselves, we won't get along with other people. When we reject ourselves, it may seem to us that others reject us as well. Relationships are a large part of our lives. How we feel about ourselves is a determining factor in our success in life and in relationships.

When I am around people who are insecure, it tends to make me feel insecure about them too. It is certainly not God's will for His children to feel insecure. Insecurity is the devil's work.

Jesus came to bring restoration to our lives.[1] One of the things Jesus came to restore is a healthy, balanced self-image.

HOW DO YOU SEE YOURSELF?

Our self-image is the inner picture we carry of ourselves. If what we see is not healthy and according to Scripture, we will suffer from fear, insecurity and various types of misconceptions about ourselves. Please note that I said "we will *suffer.*"

People who are insecure about themselves suffer in their mind and emotions, as well as in their social and spiritual lives. I know they suffer because I have talked with thousands of them. I also know because I myself have suffered in this area.

I still remember the agony of being with people and feeling they did not like me, or wanting to do things and not feeling free enough to step out and try them. Studying the Word of God and receiving His unconditional love and acceptance have brought healing to my life. It will do the same for you.

SALVATION FROM DESTRUCTION

> *So then Zacchaeus stood up and solemnly declared to the Lord, See, Lord, the half of my goods I [now] give [by way of restoration] to the poor, and if I have cheated anyone out of anything, I [now] restore four times as much.*
> *And Jesus said to him, Today is [Messianic and spiritual] salvation come to [all the members of] this household, since Zacchaeus too is a [real spiritual] son of Abraham;*
> *For the Son of Man came to seek and to save that which was lost.*
> *Luke 19:8-10*

Notice that verse 10 says "that which," not "those who." In the previous verse we see that the chief tax collector, Zacchaeus, and his household had just received salvation. They had been lost and were now saved, but their salvation was not going to end there.

The statement that follows about Jesus coming to save that which was lost tells me that He intends to save us not only from our sins, but also from everything Satan has tried to do to ruin our lives.

Each of us has a destiny and should be free to fulfill it; however, that fulfillment will not happen as long as we are insecure and have a poor self-image.

GOD APPROVES OF YOU!

> *Before I formed you in the womb I knew and approved of you [as My chosen instrument]....*
> *Jeremiah 1:5*

God never intended for us to feel bad about ourselves. He wants us to know ourselves well and yet accept ourselves.

Nobody knows us as well as God does. Yet, even though He knows us and everything about us, including all of our faults, He still approves of us and accepts us. He does not approve of our wrong behavior, but He is committed to us as individuals.

In the following pages you will have an opportunity to learn the difference between your "who" and your "do." You will discover that God can hate what you do and yet love you; He has no trouble keeping the two separated.

God is a God of hearts. He sees our heart, not just the exterior shell (the flesh) we live in that seems to get us into so much trouble. I believe if God can keep the two separated, He can teach us to do the same thing.

I believe that reading this book will be a turning point in your life. In this book you will learn to face your weaknesses and not hate yourself because of them. You will experience healing and freedom that will release you to succeed at being yourself.

1

SELF-ACCEPTANCE

1
SELF-ACCEPTANCE

**For as he thinks in his heart,
so is he....**
PROVERBS 23:7

Do you like yourself? Most
people don't like them-
selves, you know. I have many
years of experience with people,
trying to help them be whole
emotionally, mentally, spiritually
and socially. I felt it was a major breakthrough when I simply discovered that most people really don't like themselves. Some of them
know it, while others don't even have a clue that is the root of many
other problems in their life.

Self-rejection and even self-hatred are the root causes of many
relationship problems. God wants us to have great relationships. I have
found the Bible to be a book about relationships. I find teaching in it
about my relationship with God, with other people and with myself.

SEEK PEACE IN RELATIONSHIPS

> *...[Do not merely desire peaceful relations with God, with your
> fellowmen, and with yourself, but pursue, go after them!]*
> *1 Peter 3:11*

God's Word instructs us to have good relationships, but it also
teaches us how to develop and maintain those relationships.

I found this particular Scripture in *The Amplified Bible* to be very
enlightening. As I studied it, the Holy Spirit revealed to me that first
I must have peace with God. I must believe that He loves me. He
does not wait until I am perfected to love me; He loves me unconditionally and completely at all times. Second, I must *receive* His love.

Receiving is a big issue. When we receive from God, we actually
take into ourselves what He is offering. As we receive His love, we
then have love in us. Once we are filled with God's love, we can begin

loving ourselves. We can also begin giving that love back to God and bestowing it on other people.

Always remember: *we cannot give away what we don't have!*

THE LOVE OF GOD

> *...God's love has been poured out in our hearts through the*
> *Holy Spirit Who has been given to us.*
> Romans 5:5

The Bible teaches us that the love of God has been poured out in our hearts by the Holy Spirit Who has been given to us. That simply means that when the Lord, in the form of the Holy Spirit, comes to dwell in our heart because of our faith in His Son Jesus Christ, He brings love with Him, because God is love. (1 John 4:8.)

We all need to ask ourselves what we are doing with the love of God that has been freely given us. Are we rejecting it because we don't think we are valuable enough to be loved? Do we believe God is like other people who have rejected and hurt us? Or are we receiving His love by faith, believing that He is greater than our failures and weaknesses?

What kind of relationship do you have with God, with yourself and ultimately with your fellowman?

It never occurred to me that I even had a relationship with myself. It was just something I never thought of until God began teaching me in these areas. I now realize that I spend more time with myself than with anyone else, and it is vital that I get along well with me.

You are one person you never get away from.

We all know how agonizing it is to work day after day with someone we don't get along with, but at least we don't have to take that person home with us at night. But we are with us all the time, day and night. We never have one minute away from ourselves, not even one second — therefore, *it is of the utmost importance that we have peace with ourselves.*

WE CANNOT GIVE AWAY
WHAT WE DON'T HAVE

> *"...Freely you have received, freely give."*
> Matthew 10:8 NKJV

With the help of the Lord I learned to receive God's love, to love myself (in a balanced way), to love God in return and to love other people. But it was neither quick nor easy because of my personal history.

It seemed to me that I had always had difficulties in relationships, and I really did not know why. I could not find people that I liked and enjoyed who also felt the same way about me. Through God's help I finally realized what the problem was: I was trying to give away something that I did not have.

As a young believer I heard sermons about the importance of Christians loving each other, and I was sincerely trying to walk in love, but I failed continually. I needed to get God's answer hooked up with my particular problem. I had heard with my ears that God loved me, but I had not really believed it for myself. I may have believed it in general, but not personally. I had the problem, and I had the answer, but I was not making the right connection between the two.

Many times we know what our problem is, but we cannot seem to find the right answer to it. On the other hand, we often discover an answer in God's Word, but we really don't know what our problem is. God wants to reveal to us the nature of our true problems and the answer to those problems that are found in His Word. When we make the right connection between them, when we hook up the right problem with the right revelation — the devil is on his way out, and freedom is on its way in.

For example, I saw in the Bible that we were to walk in love. I knew that I had a problem with love, but I did not know that my problem had roots.

We frequently try to deal with the bad fruit in our lives and never get to the root cause of it. If the root remains, the fruit will keep coming back. No matter how many times we cut it off, eventually it will come back. This cycle is very frustrating. We are trying the best we know how, and yet it seems we never find a permanent solution to our miseries.

I was desperately attempting to display loving behavior, but I had failed to receive God's love; therefore, I could not give love away. I did not have any to give.

LOVE YOUR NEIGHBOR AS YOU LOVE YOURSELF

> *For the whole Law [concerning human relationships] is complied with in the one precept, You shall love your neighbor as [you do] yourself.*
> *Galatians 5:14*

While I was seeking answers to my problems, the Holy Spirit opened up to me Galatians 5:14 in a way I had never seen or heard before. I was experiencing marriage problems. My husband and I were not getting along — it seemed we couldn't agree on anything, we had strife almost continually. It was affecting our children in an adverse way. All the anxiety and turmoil were affecting my health. *I had to have some answers!*

THE ANSWER IS LOVE

> *There is no fear in love; but perfect love casteth out fear....*
> *1 John 4:18 KJV*

When the Holy Spirit revealed this Scripture to me, I asked myself, could it be possible? Was I hearing God right — could it be as simple as "Jesus loves me, *this I know,* for the Bible tells me so"? I had a lot of fears in my life, and 1 John 4:18 was telling me that perfect love would cast out fear.

I had tried walking in "perfect love" and had failed daily. I thought "perfect love" referred to my loving others perfectly. I was now beginning to see that perfect love was God's love for me — He is the only One Who can love perfectly.

God's love is perfect even when we are not!

LOVED TO LOVE OTHERS

> *May Christ through your faith [actually] dwell (settle down, abide, make His permanent home) in your hearts! May you be rooted deep in love and founded securely on love,*
> *That you may have the power and be strong to apprehend and grasp with all the saints [God's devoted people, the experience of that love] what is the breadth and length and height and depth [of it].*
> *Ephesians 3:17,18*

As I meditated on these Scriptures and others like them, I felt like a blind person who was seeing for the first time. *My problem was a lack of love.* I had never received proper love in my life; therefore, I had never learned to properly love myself. I didn't even like myself, let alone love myself.

If nobody else loves us, we don't see why we should love ourselves. If others don't love us, we think we must not be worth loving.

We should love ourselves — not in a selfish, self-centered way that produces a lifestyle of self-indulgence, but in a balanced, godly way, a way that simply affirms God's creation as essentially good and right. We may be flawed by the years and the unfortunate experiences we have undergone, but that does not mean we are worthless and good for nothing but the trash can.

We must have the kind of love that says, "I can love what God can love. I don't love everything I do, but I accept myself, because God accepts me." We must develop the kind of mature love that says, "I know I need to change, and I want to change. In fact, I believe God is changing me daily, but in the meanwhile I will not reject what God accepts. I will accept myself as I am right now, knowing that I will not always remain this way."

Our faith gives us hope for the future. As He did with the Israelites, God will help us conquer our enemies (our "hangups") little by little. (Deuteronomy 7:22.) He will change us from glory to glory as we continue to look into His Word. (2 Corinthians 3:18 KJV.) He is the Author and Finisher of our faith. (Hebrews 12:2 KJV.) He has begun a good work in us, and He will complete it and bring it to its final fulfillment. (Philippians 1:6.)

Once we receive God's love and begin to love and accept ourselves, it greatly improves our relationship with Him. Until we accept His love, the cycle is incomplete. We can love Him only because He first loved us. (1 John 4:19.)

We all know how frustrating it is to attempt to give a gift to someone who keeps refusing to take it. I love to surprise people and give them something they want or need. I have had the experience of planning a surprise, going shopping, spending my money, getting everything ready, and yet when I gave my gift, the person was so insecure they did not know how to simply receive my gift graciously.

Insecurity and feelings of unworthiness keep us from being able to receive very well. We may feel that we must earn or deserve everything we get. We may think, "Why would someone want to just *give* me something?" We may become suspicious: "What is their motive? What do they want from me? What are they after?"

There are times when I try to give something to someone and have to spend so much time and energy convincing them I really do want them to have it, that the situation becomes downright embarrassing. I just want them to take it! I want them to show their appreciation for my gift by graciously receiving it and enjoying it.

If we as humans feel that way, how much more does God feel that way when He tries to give us His love, grace and mercy, and we refuse it because of a false sense of humility or unworthiness? When God reaches out to love us, He is attempting to start a cycle that will bless not only us but also many others.

God's plan is this: He wants us to receive His love, love ourselves in a balanced and godly way, generously love Him in return, and finally love all the people who come into our lives.

We have failed to follow that plan for years. We are not even loving others with our own love, much less with God's love. Remember, we did not have any love with which to love anyone until God first loved us!

ACCEPTANCE OR REJECTION?

And God saw everything that He had made, and behold, it was very good (suitable, pleasant) and He approved it completely. And there was evening and there was morning, a sixth day.
Genesis 1:31

Rejecting ourselves does not change us, it actually multiplies our problems. Acceptance causes us to face reality and then begin to deal with it. We cannot deal with anything as long as we are refusing to accept it or denying its reality.

Webster's II New College Dictionary defines *accept* in part as: "**1.** To receive (something offered), esp. willingly. **2.** To admit to a group or place. **3. a.** To consider as usual, proper, or right. **b.** To consider as true."[1]

I notice from this definition that acceptance involves the will. If I apply this definition to self-acceptance, I see that I can choose or not choose to accept myself. God is offering me the opportunity to accept myself as I am, but I have a free will and can refuse to do so if I so choose. I also see from this definition that when something is accepted, it is viewed as usual, proper or right.

People who reject themselves do so because they cannot see themselves as proper or right. They only see their flaws and weaknesses, not their beauty and strength. This is an unbalanced attitude, one that was probably instilled by authority figures in the past who majored on what was weak and wrong rather than on what was strong and right.

The word *acceptance* from the same dictionary is defined in part as "approval" and "agreement."[2] If we are having problems accepting ourselves as we are, I suggest that we need to get into agreement with God that what He created is good — and that includes us.

In Amos 3:3 we read, *Do two walk together except they make an appointment and have agreed?* To walk with God, we must agree with God. He says He loves us and accepts us; therefore, if we agree with Him, we can no longer hate and reject ourselves.

We need to agree with God that when He created us, He created something good.

Once again let me emphasize that I realize everything we do is not good, but at this point we are discussing ourselves, not our behavior. Later in the book we will discuss in detail how God views what we do; right now in this beginning chapter we are more concerned with who we are in God's sight.

You may be at the same place I was when God began revealing these principles to me. You see the things in yourself that need to be changed, and it is very difficult for you to think or say, "I accept myself." You feel that to do so would be to accept all that is wrong with you, but that is not the case.

I personally don't believe we can even begin the process of change until this issue is settled in our individual lives.

CHANGE REQUIRES CORRECTION

For the Lord corrects and disciplines everyone whom He loves, and He punishes, even scourges, every son whom He accepts and welcomes to His heart and cherishes.
Hebrews 12:6

This truth about God's correction and discipline of those He loves is verified by Jesus Himself in Revelation 3:19 when He says: *Those whom I [dearly and tenderly] love, I tell their faults and convict and convince and reprove and chasten [I discipline and instruct them]. So be enthusiastic and in earnest and burning with zeal and repent [changing your mind and attitude].*

Change requires correction — people who do not know they are loved have a very difficult time receiving correction. Correction does no good at all if it is not received.

In dealing with my children and hundreds of employees over the years, I have discovered that correction must be given in love. In other words, for my correction to be successful, the people I am correcting must know that I love them and care about them.

I can spend a lot of time correcting someone, but my time is wasted unless that individual receives what I have said. In the same way, in order for God to change us, He must correct us. We won't receive His correction properly if we don't have a revelation concerning

His love for us. We may hear His correction and even agree with it, but it will only make us feel angry or condemned unless we know it is ultimately going to bring about the change that is needed in our life.

BE ASSURED OF GOD'S LOVE FOR YOU

> *For I am persuaded beyond doubt (am sure) that neither death nor life, nor angels nor principalities, nor things impending and threatening nor things to come, nor powers, Nor height nor depth, nor anything else in all creation will be able to separate us from the love of God which is in Christ Jesus our Lord.*
> *Romans 8:38,39*

We cannot trust unless we believe we are loved. To grow up in God and be changed, we must trust Him. Often He will lead us in ways that we cannot understand, and during those times we must have a tight grip on His love for us.

The Apostle Paul was convinced that nothing would ever be able to separate us from the love of God in Christ Jesus. We need to have that same absolute assurance of God's undying love for us individually.

Accept God's love for you and make that love the basis for your love and acceptance of yourself. Receive His affirmation, knowing that you are changing and becoming all that He desires you to be. Then start enjoying yourself — where you are — on your way to full spiritual maturity.

2

YOUR SELF-IMAGE AFFECTS YOUR FUTURE

2
YOUR SELF-IMAGE AFFECTS YOUR FUTURE

We have already established that insecurity caused by a poor self-image affects all of our relationships. It also greatly affects our future.

And [the cripple] bowed himself and said, What is your servant, that you should look upon such a dead dog as I am?
2 SAMUEL 9:8

If you have a poor self-image, it has already adversely affected your past, but you can be healed and not allow the past to repeat itself. Let go of what lies behind, including any negative ways you have felt about yourself, and press on toward the good things God has in store for you.

GOD HAS PLANS FOR EACH OF US

For we are God's [own] handiwork (His workmanship), recreated in Christ Jesus, [born anew] that we may do those good works which God predestined (planned beforehand) for us [taking paths which He prepared ahead of time], that we should walk in them [living the good life which He prearranged and made ready for us to live].
Ephesians 2:10

God has a good plan for each one of us, but not all of us experience it. Many times we live far below the standard that God intends for us to enjoy.

For years I did not exercise my rights and privileges as a child of God. This occurred for two reasons. The first was, I did not even know I had any rights or privileges. Although I was a Christian and believed I would go to heaven when I died, I did not know that anything could be done about my past, present or future. The second reason I lived far below the level of life God intended for me was very simply the wrong way I perceived and felt about myself. I had a poor self-image, and it affected my day-to-day living, as well as my outlook for the future.

GOD HAS PLANS FOR YOU!

> *For I know the thoughts and plans that I have for you, says*
> *the Lord, thoughts and plans for welfare and peace and not*
> *for evil, to give you hope in your final outcome.*
> *Jeremiah 29:11*

If you have a poor self-image, as I did, I recommend that you read the story of Mephibosheth, which is found in the ninth chapter of 2 Samuel. It greatly affected my life, and I believe it will do the same for you. It will help you see not only why you are living far below the level that God intends for you now, but also why you are in danger of missing out on what He has in mind for you in the future.

"IS THERE ANYONE I CAN BLESS?"

> *And David said, Is there still anyone left of the house of Saul*
> *to whom I may show kindness for Jonathan's sake?*
> *2 Samuel 9:1*

Mephibosheth was the grandson of King Saul and the son of Jonathan, who had been a close covenant friend to David. Jonathan and his father Saul had both been killed in battle, and David was now king.

David had a desire to bless someone in Saul's family for Jonathan's sake. He inquired as to whether there was anyone left of the household of Saul to whom he could show kindness. One of his servants reported that Mephibosheth was alive and living in a town called Lo-debar.

The name *Lo-debar* means "pastureless."[1] In an agricultural society, a place without pastures was probably a place of poverty. Why would a king's grandson be living in such a place? Why hadn't he come to the palace claiming his rights and privileges as an heir of King Saul, not to mention his rights and privileges as the son of Jonathan, who had covenant relationship with the present king? He surely understood covenant relationship; everyone did in those days. He knew that the covenant between his father Jonathan and David the king extended to their children and heirs.

In ancient Israel, when two people entered into a covenant relationship, everything each of them possessed was made available to the other. The covenant relationship also meant that they would help one another, fight for one another, do anything necessary to meet each other's needs. Yet Mephibosheth, the rightful heir of Jonathan, King David's covenant partner, was living in poverty. Why? The reason goes back to the last days of the reign of King Saul, Mephibosheth's grandfather.

When news came to the palace that Saul and Jonathan had been killed in battle, Mephibosheth was just a child. Hearing the dreadful news, his nurse ran from the palace with him in her arms, fearing that David might try to take vengeance on the boy because of the way David had been treated by King Saul. During her escape, Mephibosheth fell and was crippled in his legs as a result. (2 Samuel 4:4.)

When David sent for Mephibosheth, he fell down before the king and displayed fear. David told him not to fear, that he intended to show him kindness. Mephibosheth's response is an important example of the kind of poor self-image we all need to overcome.

THE DEAD-DOG IMAGE

> *And Mephibosheth son of Jonathan, the son of Saul, came to David and fell on his face and did obeisance. David said, Mephibosheth! And he answered, Behold your servant! David said to him, Fear not, for I will surely show you kindness for Jonathan your father's sake, and will restore to you all the land of Saul your father [grandfather], and you shall eat at my table always.*

And [the cripple] bowed himself and said, What is your
servant, that you should look upon such a dead dog as I am?
2 Samuel 9:6–8

Mephibosheth had a poor self-image, a dead-dog image. He did not think very well of himself. Instead of seeing himself as the rightful heir to his father's and grandfather's legacy, he saw himself as someone who would be rejected. If this were not true, he would have already gone to the palace long ago on his own to claim his inheritance.

A poor self-image causes us to operate in fear instead of faith. We look at what is wrong with us instead of what is right with Jesus. He has taken our wrongness and given us His righteousness. (2 Corinthians 5:21.) We need to walk in the reality of that truth.

When I saw this passage, I realized that I also had a dead-dog image, and it was hindering me from being all I could be and having all I could have in life. I started changing my attitude toward myself. It took time and a lot of help from the Holy Spirit, but I determined that I would not live below the blessings Jesus had provided for me.

God's Word says that because of His covenant with us, we can be the head and not the tail, above only and not beneath. (Deuteronomy 28:13.) I am sure that, like me, you have been the tail long enough. It is time to take a stand and start receiving your rightful inheritance.

David blessed Mephibosheth. He gave him servants and land and provided for all of his needs. The story ends by saying, *So Mephibosheth dwelt in Jerusalem, for he ate continually at the king's table, [even though] he was lame in both feet* (2 Samuel 9:13).

I absolutely love the end of the story. I relate Mephibosheth's lameness to our own weaknesses. We may also fellowship and eat with our King Jesus — even though we have faults and weaknesses. We still have a covenant with God, sealed and ratified in the blood of Jesus

Christ. Blood covenant was, and still is, one of the strongest agreements that can be made between two parties.

We offer God what we have, and He gives us what He has. He takes all of our sins, faults, weaknesses and failures, and gives us His ability, His righteousness, and His strength. He takes our poverty, and gives us His riches. He takes our diseases and sicknesses, and gives us His healing and health. He takes our messed up, failure-filled past, and gives us the hope of a bright future.

In ourselves we are nothing, our own righteousness is like filthy rags or a polluted garment. (Isaiah 64:6.) But in Christ we have a future worth looking forward to. The term "in Christ" very simply stated means that we have placed our faith in Him concerning every aspect of our lives. We are in covenant with Almighty God. What an awesome thought!

ARE YOU A GRASSHOPPER?

There we saw the Nephilim [or giants], the sons of Anak, who come from the giants; and we were in our own sight as grasshoppers, and so we were in their sight.
Numbers 13:33

Another story that greatly affected me is found in Numbers 13. Moses sent twelve men to scout out the Promised Land to see if it was good or bad. Ten of the men came back with what the Bible refers to as "an evil report." (Numbers 13:32.) Only two of the scouts, Caleb and Joshua, had the attitude God wanted them to have.

When the twelve scouts returned from their journey, *They told Moses, We came to the land to which you sent us; surely it flows with milk and honey...* (Numbers 13:27). Then they continued: *But the people who dwell there are strong, and the cities are fortified and very large; moreover, there we saw the sons of Anak [of great stature and courage]* (Numbers 13:28). In other words, "The land is good, but there are giants in it!" The fear of the giants prevented God's people from entering the land that He had promised to give them. They only saw the giants; they failed to see God.

It wasn't really the giants that defeated these people, it was their poor self-image. It was their wrong attitude toward themselves. They saw others as giants and themselves as grasshoppers.

Joshua and Caleb were the only ones who had a proper attitude toward the land. They said to Moses and the people, ...*Let us go up at once and possess it; we are well able to conquer it* (Numbers 13:30). In the end, they were the only ones who were allowed by God to go into the Promised Land.

God had a glorious future planned for *all* of the Israelites, but *all* of them did not enter in to that future — only the ones who had a proper attitude toward God and toward themselves.

"Let us go up at once and possess it; we are well able to conquer it." What a victory statement! What a great attitude!

This event happened thousands of years ago, and it still inspires me today. We can have a dead-dog image or a grasshopper image, but they both adversely affect our future. We see the proof in the stories of Mephibosheth and the twelve scouts. No matter what God has planned for us, we will never experience it unless we get into agreement with Him.

God does not have a bad attitude toward you — you should not have one toward yourself! Shake off the past and set your sights on the future. The Apostle Paul wanted to do things right, and yet he realized that he was growing and learning and would not always manifest 100 percent perfection.

PRESS ON! ───────────────────────────────

Not that I have now attained [this ideal], or have already been made perfect, but I press on to lay hold of (grasp) and

make my own, that for which Christ Jesus (the Messiah) has laid hold of me and made me His own.
Philippians 3:12

In the next verse, Paul went on to say that he forgot what lay behind and strained forward to what lay ahead.

We see this principle in many places in God's Holy Word. The prophet Isaiah had the same revelation when he brought forth the message of the Lord: *Do not [earnestly] remember the former things; neither consider the things of old. Behold, I am doing a new thing!...* (Isaiah 43:18,19).

I believe God has led you to read this book because He wants to do a new thing in you and in your life.

Almost every one of us could use some improvement in our self-image. It takes time to grasp the hope for ourselves that God has for us.

To realize how much hope God has for me, all I need to do is remember what I was like when God called me into full-time ministry. I certainly was not the kind of material the world would have picked to be doing what I am doing today. As a matter of fact, I firmly believe most people would have given up on me.

It is so wonderful and comforting to know that when everyone else only sees our faults, God still sees our possibilities.

When God began using me to minister to others, I still had a lot of bad habits in my own life. I needed a lot of refining. I sincerely loved God, and I wanted to do what was right, but I possessed very little revelation about any of His precepts. I knew the Ten Commandments, and I went to church and tried to be "good." I added in some "good works" and hoped it would be enough to get me into "the pearly gates," but I had no real victory in my daily life.

I was sincere, but poverty-stricken concerning real truth. I had multiple problems. I had been sexually abused as a child for many years, and the effects were still devastating me. I had also been hurt in several personal relationships and had no real understanding of what love even was.

I had a shame-based, guilt-ridden personality that stemmed from the abuse, which was carried into virtually every area of my life. I certainly did not like myself. I definitely had a very poor self-image. I was insecure "to the max" and very fearful. Outwardly I presented myself as independent and self-sufficient, not needing anyone, not caring what others thought of me. To those who didn't know me, I must have seemed very bold and aggressive. My outer life, however, did not match my inner life. Inwardly, I was a mess. Yet God filled me with His Holy Spirit and let me know that He wanted to use me to minister to others.

The Lord did not wait for me to get all fixed up before He got involved with me. He started with me where I was then and has been responsible for getting me to where I am today. I am convinced that He will do the same for you.

GOD WILL MEET YOU WHERE YOU ARE

And God heard the voice of the youth, and the angel of God called to Hagar out of heaven and said to her, What troubles you, Hagar? Fear not, for God has heard the voice of the youth where he is.
Genesis 21:17

In the Bible we find that when people were in trouble, God met them where they were and helped them. Thank God He does not wait for us to manage to get to Him — but He comes to us!

Sarah's handmaid Hagar and her son Ishmael had been cast out by Abraham and Sarah and were facing death in the desert. God had told

34

Abraham to do as Sarah suggested and separate Ishmael (the son of their own effort) and Isaac (the son of promise).

But God was not finished with Ishmael. He was not trashing him, as it must have seemed at the moment, but was moving him into another chapter of his life.

Ishmael could have definitely been looked upon as a mistake. Earlier, God had told Abram and Sarai (later renamed Abraham and Sarah) that He would give them a child. They, like many of us, got tired of waiting on God and began developing their own plan. They made a mistake, but God did not stop working with them.

Sarai gave her handmaid Hagar to Abram to be his secondary wife. She asked him to have intercourse with Hagar, since she herself was barren. She reasoned that by this action God would give them the promised child. This was not God's plan at all, and it actually caused a great deal of trouble, as we read in Genesis 16-18. As we study these chapters it seems that everybody was making mistakes. But God obviously knew their hearts because He was standing by to bring correction and to redeem the mess they were creating.

God often makes miracles out of mistakes. The abuse that was heaped upon me as a child was definitely a mistake and should have never happened. It was a mistake not only for me, but for everyone involved. However, because God is so great, He has taken that mistake and made a ministry out of it, one that is helping others. God met me where I was, and even though other people would have rejected me as unfit for the ministry, God accepted me.

GOD CHOOSES THE UNLIKELY — LIKE ME AND YOU! ────

...God selected (deliberately chose) what in the world is foolish to put the wise to shame, and what the world calls weak to put the strong to shame.

*And God also selected (deliberately chose) what in the world is
lowborn and insignificant and branded and treated with
contempt, even the things that are nothing, that He might
depose and bring to nothing the things that are,
So that no mortal man should [have pretense for glorying
and] boast in the presence of God.
1 Corinthians 1:27-29*

God purposely chooses those who are the most unlikely candidates for the job. By doing so, He has a wide open door to show His grace, mercy and power to change human lives. When God uses someone like me or many others He is using, we realize that our source is not in ourselves but in Him alone: *[This is] because the foolish thing [that has its source in] God is wiser than men, and the weak thing [that springs] from God is stronger than men* (1 Corinthians 1:25).

Each of us has a destiny, and there is absolutely no excuse not to fulfill it. We cannot use our weakness as an excuse, because God says that His strength is made perfect in weakness. (2 Corinthians 12:9.) We cannot use the past as an excuse because God tells us through the Apostle Paul that if any person is in Christ, he is a new creature; old things have passed away, and all things have become new. (2 Corinthians 5:17.)

How God sees us is not the problem, it is how we see ourselves that keeps us from succeeding. Each of us can succeed at being everything God intends us to be.

Spend some time with yourself and take an inventory of how you feel about yourself. What is your image of yourself? What kind of picture do you carry in yourself of yourself? When you get it out and look at it, do you resemble a dead dog or a grasshopper? Do you see a hopeless creature that nobody loves? Or do you see yourself recreated in God's image, resurrected to a brand new life that is just waiting for you to claim it?

3

"I'M OK, AND I'M ON MY WAY!"

3
"I'M OK, AND I'M ON MY WAY!"

I have not arrived, and neither has anyone else. We are all in the process of becoming. For much of my life I felt that I would never be OK until I arrived, but I have learned that is not the truth. My heart desires to be all God wants me to be, and I want to be like Jesus. My flesh does not always cooperate with me.

And I am convinced and sure of this very thing, that He Who began a good work in you will continue until the day of Jesus Christ [right up to the time of His return], developing [that good work] and perfecting and bringing it to full completion in you.
PHILIPPIANS 1:6

In Romans 7, Paul said the good things he wanted to do, he could not do; and the evil things he did not want to do, he always found himself doing. He said he felt wretched. I can relate to that — how about you? In verse 24 he cried out, ...*Who will release and deliver me from [the shackles of] this body of death?* Then in the following verse, as if he had received an answer that was a revelation to him, he said, *O thank God! [He will!] through Jesus Christ (the Anointed One) our Lord!...*

Yes, we all have a way to go. I was distraught about how far I had to go, and it seemed Satan reminded me of it daily, sometimes even hourly. I carried a constant sense of failure, a feeling that I just was not what I needed to be, that I was not doing good enough, that I should try harder — and yet when I did try harder, I only failed more.

I have now adopted a new attitude: "I am not where I need to be, but thank God I am not where I used to be; I'm OK, and I'm on my way!"

KEEP ON WALKING! ─────────────────

But the path of the [uncompromisingly] just and righteous is like the light of dawn, that shines more and more (brighter

and clearer) until [it reaches its full strength and glory in] the
perfect day [to be prepared].
Proverbs 4:18

I now know with all my heart that God is not angry with me because I have not arrived. He is pleased that I am pressing on, that I am staying on the path. If you and I will just "keep on keeping on," God will be pleased with our progress.

Keep walking the walk. A walk is something taken one step at a time. This is an important thing to remember.

If I invited you to take a walk, you would think I was crazy if I became angry after the first few steps because we had not yet arrived at our destination. We can understand ordinary things like this, and yet we have a difficult time understanding that God expects it to take some time for us to grow spiritually.

We don't think there is something wrong with one-year-old children because they cannot walk perfectly. They fall down frequently, but we pick them up, love them, bandage them if necessary, and keep working with them. Surely our awesome God can do even more for us than we do for our children.

KEEPING IN BALANCE

Be well balanced (temperate, sober of mind), be vigilant and
cautious at all times; for that enemy of yours, the devil, roams
around like a lion roaring [in fierce hunger], seeking someone
to seize upon and devour.
1 Peter 5:8

It is very important to maintain balance in all things, for if we don't we open a door for Satan.

We have been considering how to have a good self-image. One way we do that is by realizing that we have not arrived at perfection, that we have some growing to do, but that in the meantime we are OK. It is true that we have to keep pressing on, but thank God we don't have to hate and reject ourselves while we are trying to get to our destination.

What is a normal, healthy Christian attitude toward self? Here are a few thoughts that reflect that kind of wholesome, God-centered self-image:

1. I know God created me, and He loves me.

2. I have faults and weaknesses, and I want to change. I believe God is working in my life. He is changing me bit by bit, day by day. While He is doing so, I can still enjoy myself and my life.

3. Everyone has faults, so I am not a complete failure just because I am not perfect.

4. I am going to work with God to overcome my weaknesses, but I realize that I will always have something to deal with; therefore, I will not become discouraged when God convicts me of areas in my life that need improvement.

5. I want to make people happy and have them like me, but my sense of worth is not dependent on what others think of me. Jesus has already affirmed my value by His willingness to die for me.

6. I will not be controlled by what people think, say or do. Even if they totally reject me, I will survive. God has promised never to reject me or condemn me as long as I keep believing. (John 6:29.)

7. No matter how often I fail, I will not give up, because God is with me to strengthen and sustain me. He has promised never to leave me or forsake me. (Hebrews 13:5.)

8. I like myself. I don't like everything I do, and I want to change — but I refuse to reject myself.

9. I am right with God through Jesus Christ.

10. God has a good plan for my life. I am going to fulfill my destiny and be all I can be for His glory. I have God-given gifts and talents, and I intend to use them to help others.

11. I am nothing, and yet I am everything! In myself I am nothing, and yet in Jesus I am everything I need to be.

12. I can do all things I need to do, everything that God calls me to do, through His Son Jesus Christ. (Philippians 4:13.)

Here are some additional suggestions to help you develop and maintain a balanced attitude and a healthy self-image:

1. Always reject and hate your sin, but don't reject yourself.

2. Be quick to repent.

3. Be honest with God and yourself, about yourself.

4. When God gives you light, don't fear it.

5. Stop saying negative, downgrading things about yourself, but don't boast either.

6. Don't have an exaggerated opinion of your own importance, but don't think you are insignificant.

7. Don't always assume when things go wrong that it is your fault. But don't be afraid to admit it, if you are wrong.

8. Beware of having yourself on your mind too much. Don't meditate excessively on what you have done right or what you have done wrong. Both of these activities keep your mind on you! Keep your thoughts centered on Christ and His principles: *You will guard him and keep him in perfect and constant peace whose mind [both its inclination and its character] is stayed on You...* (Isaiah 26:3).

9. Take good care of yourself physically. Do the best you can with what God gave you to work with — but don't be excessive or vain about your appearance.

10. Learn all you can, but don't allow your education to become a point of pride. God does not use us because of our education, but because of our heart toward Him.

11. Realize that your gifts and talents are a gift, not something you have manufactured yourself. Don't look down on people who cannot do what you can do.

12. Don't despise your weaknesses — they keep you dependent upon God.

"HOW CAN I CHANGE?"

> *Do not be conformed to this world (this age), [fashioned after and adapted to its external, superficial customs], but be transformed (changed) by the [entire] renewal of your mind [by its new ideals and its new attitude]....*
> *Romans 12:2*

Change does not come through struggle, human effort without God, frustration, self-hatred, self-rejection, guilt or works of the flesh.

Change in our lives comes as a result of having our minds renewed by the Word of God. As we agree with God and really believe that what He says is true, it gradually begins to manifest itself in us. We begin to think differently, then we begin to talk differently, and finally we begin to act differently. This is a process that develops in stages, and we must always remember that while it is taking place we can still have the attitude, "I'm OK, and I'm on my way!"

Enjoy yourself while you are changing. Enjoy where you are on the way to where you are going. Enjoy the journey! Don't waste all of your "now time" trying to rush into the future. Remember, tomorrow will have troubles of its own. (Matthew 6:34.)

Today you may be wrestling with a bad temper and thinking if
you could just get freedom in that area, everything would be all right.
The thing is, you may have forgotten that God will then reveal something else that needs to be dealt with, and you will be back in the
same frame of mind again, thinking, "If only I didn't have this
problem, I could be happy."

We must learn to look at these things in a new way.

A NEW AND LIVING WAY

> *By this fresh (new) and living way which He initiated and
> dedicated and opened for us through the separating curtain
> (veil of the Holy of Holies), that is, through His flesh.*
> *Hebrews 10:20*

Under the Old Covenant, people had to follow the Law; when they
made mistakes they had to make sacrifices to atone for them. There
were a great number of laws, too many for anyone to manage to keep
them all. The result was works, works, works — people trying and
failing; feeling guilty and trying harder; failing again and making sacrifices.
It was a never-ending cycle that drained all the life from the people.

The Law came to the people on two stone tablets, given to Moses
by God. It made the people's hearts hard and stony as they desperately
tried to keep it.

The Law, the "dispensation of death," was replaced by "the
dispensation of the Spirit," a new and living way.

LAW OR SPIRIT?

> *Now if the dispensation of death engraved in letters on stone
> [the ministration of the Law], was inaugurated with such
> glory and splendor that the Israelites were not able to look
> steadily at the face of Moses because of its brilliance, [a glory]
> that was to fade and pass away,*

Why should not the dispensation of the Spirit [this spiritual ministry whose task it is to cause men to obtain and be governed by the Holy Spirit] be attended with much greater and more splendid glory?
2 Corinthians 3:7,8

Living under the Law actually ministers death rather than life. To me, "living under the Law" means that I feel I must do everything perfectly; otherwise, I am in trouble with God. It means rules and regulations, with no freedom. I lived under the Law for years, and it stole all my peace and joy. I was alive, and yet I was filled with death.

Death in this sense actually means every kind of misery. Legalistic living makes people tense and rigid. They know practically nothing about mercy; they neither receive it from God nor give it to others.

While I was trying to learn to walk in love, I realized I was not a very merciful person. Once again God taught me that I could not give away something I did not have. I was not receiving His mercy for my failures; therefore, I did not have any mercy to give to other people. I tried to follow all the rules and regulations: ones that had been handed down to me, those that the Church had issued and all the thousands I had allowed Satan to program my mind with. These were not even scriptural, they were just things to feel guilty about.

God gave Moses ten commandments. I once read that by the time Jesus came, the religious leaders had turned those ten commandments into approximately 2,200 different rules and regulations for the people to follow. I don't know for sure if they had 2,200 or not, but I do know they had more than any person could possibly handle.

Some people have greater tendencies toward legalism than others. Even our natural temperament can contribute toward perfectionism and legalism. But we must remember that where there is legalism, there is also death.

Jesus said He came to give life. (John 10:10.) The new dispensation was one whereby people were to be governed not by Law, but by the Spirit of God. *It was a new way of living!* It included mercy for failure, forgiveness for sin, and replacement of sacrifices with faith in Jesus Christ.

It was almost too good to be true. It was simple, and for many people it was too simple. They just could not believe it. They kept working at trying to impress God with their goodness. The Bible says that we are justified through faith, not by works. (Ephesians 2:8,9.) Any attempt to obtain justification and righteousness any other way only frustrates us and wears us out.

WE ARE THROUGH WITH LEGALISM AND READY FOR A NEW LIFE!

> *But now we are discharged from the Law and have terminated all intercourse with it, having died to what once restrained and held us captive. So now we serve not under [obedience to] the old code of written regulations, but [under obedience to the promptings] of the Spirit in newness [of life].*
> *Romans 7:6*

We see again that serving God under the New Covenant brings newness of life. It really is an entirely new way of living, and we must have our minds renewed to it. We will have to learn to think differently — about ourselves and about what God expects of us.

THE JOY OF PROGRESS

> *...if only I may finish my course with joy....*
> *Acts 20:24*

The Apostle Paul wanted to be all God wanted him to be, and he desired to do all God wanted him to do — but he wanted to do it with joy.

We should learn to be joyful about our progress, not depressed about how far we still have to go. We must learn to look at the positive, not the negative.

One of the side effects of legalism is that people can never be satisfied unless they keep all the Law. If they fail in one point, they are guilty of all. (James 2:10.) One of the benefits of the New Covenant is the fact that we can be satisfied during the entire journey. Our satisfaction is not to be found in our performance, but in Jesus Himself.

In John 10:10 Jesus said He came that we might have and enjoy our lives. In that same verse He said, *The thief comes only in order to steal and kill and destroy....* The thief He was actually referring to is legalism or a legalistic approach to God. It steals everything from us and gives us nothing in return but guilt and misery. By Law we cannot be righteous, nor have peace and joy. Through Jesus all these things are ours as free gifts, given by God's grace, not earned by our works. We receive them by believing.

LIVE IN JOY, PEACE AND HOPE

> *May the God of your hope so fill you with all joy and peace in believing [through the experience of your faith] that by the power of the Holy Spirit you may abound and be overflowing (bubbling over) with hope.*
> *Romans 15:13*

I remember an evening when I was feeling strongly dissatisfied and discontented. I went to a promise box someone had given me. A promise box is a little container filled with Scriptures. Its purpose is for the believer to be able to draw out a Scripture that will recall one of God's promises whenever there is a need. Well, I felt I needed something, but I was not sure what it was. I had no peace or joy and was absolutely miserable.

I pulled out a card with Romans 15:13 printed on it, and it was indeed "a word in season" for me. (Isaiah 50:4.) My problem was simple, I was doubting instead of believing. I was doubting God's unconditional love, doubting that I could hear from Him, doubting His call on my life, doubting that He was pleased with me. I was filled with doubt...doubt...doubt. When I saw the problem, I got back into faith and out of doubt. My joy and peace returned immediately.

I have found the same thing to be true again and again in my life. When joy and peace seem to be gone, I check my believing — usually it is gone also. It stands to reason then that doubting ourselves will also steal our joy and peace.

I can remember years of my life when most of my relationship with myself was one of doubting myself. I doubted my decisions; I doubted my appearance; I doubted whether I was really being led by the Holy Spirit; I doubted whether I was doing the right thing or saying the right thing; I doubted whether I was in any way pleasing God or anyone else. I knew I was not pleased with myself, so how could anyone else be pleased with me?

I am so glad those years of misery are behind me. Now I practice Galatians 5:1: *In [this] freedom Christ has made us free [and completely liberated us]; stand fast then, and do not be hampered and held ensnared and submit again to a yoke of slavery [which you have once put off].* I had such a bondage of legalism in my life that I will probably always have to stand firmly against it. Now I recognize it and its symptoms — and that knowledge keeps me resisting Satan and enjoying freedom in Christ.

We can be free to believe that we are indeed OK and on our way — not perfected yet, but pressing on. We can be free to enjoy life, enjoy God and enjoy ourselves.

4

HAVE YOU
LOST YOURSELF?

4
HAVE YOU LOST YOURSELF?

How can we succeed at being ourselves if we don't know ourselves? Life is like a maze sometimes, and it is easy to get lost. Everyone, it seems, expects something different from us. There is pressure coming at us from every direction to keep others happy and meet their needs.

We put a large amount of emotional and mental energy into studying the important people in our lives and trying to decide what they want from us. We then attempt to become what they want us to

Having gifts (faculties, talents, qualities) that differ according to the grace given us, let us use them: [He whose gift is] prophecy, [let him prophesy] according to the proportion of his faith; [He whose gift is] practical service, let him give himself to serving; he who teaches, to his teaching; He who exhorts (encourages), to his exhortation; he who contributes, let him do it in simplicity and liberality; he who gives aid and superintends, with zeal and singleness of mind; he who does acts of mercy, with genuine cheerfulness and joyful eagerness.
ROMANS 12:6-8

be. In the process, we may lose ourselves. We may fail to discover what God wants, or what His intention is for us. We may try to please everyone else and yet not be pleased ourselves.

In my own life, for years I tried to be so many things that I wasn't, I got myself totally confused. I finally realized I didn't know what I was supposed to be like. Somewhere in the process of trying to meet all the demands placed upon me by myself and others, I lost Joyce Meyer. I had to get off the merry-go-round, so to speak, and ask myself some serious questions like: "Who am I living for? Why am I doing all these things? Have I become a people-pleaser? Am I really in God's will for my life? What do I want to do with my life? What do I really believe I am gifted and anointed for?"

I felt the pressure of trying to be like my husband. Dave has always been very calm, stable, easygoing and free from any worry or care. I knew that was the right way to be, and so I tried very hard to be like him. I, on the other hand, was aggressive. I made quick decisions. I wasn't as stable in my moods as Dave was, and I tended to worry when we had problems.

I felt the pressure to be like my friends and peers. My pastor's wife is very sweet-natured. When I was around her, I felt I needed to be sweeter.

I felt the pressure to be like my friend. She was very creative; she cooked, sewed, painted, wallpapered, gardened and seemed to be all the things I wasn't — so I tried to be like her.

Actually I was trying to be like so many people at once that I got lost.

Have you also lost yourself? Are you frustrated from trying to meet all the demands of other people while feeling unfulfilled yourself? If so, you will have to take a stand and be determined to find yourself and then succeed at being yourself. If you buy into the world's strategy, something will be screaming at you from every side.

For instance, your mother may want you to be gentle, kind and loving. Your father may want you to be strong, confident and aggressive. Your mother may want you to visit her more often. Your father may want you to spend more time on the golf course with him. Your friends may want you to continue your education. Your doctor or physical trainer may want you to exercise three times a week. Your spouse may want you to be more available, and your children may need you to be more involved in their school activities. Your boss may want you to work overtime, your church may need you to usher and help with the Easter play, the music director may insist that you sing in the choir, and your neighbors may want you to cut your lawn more often!

Have you ever felt that you could not be everything that everybody wanted you to be? Have you ever known deep down inside that you really needed to say "no" to a lot of people — but the fear of displeasing them had your mouth saying, "I'll try," while your heart was screaming, "I can't do it!"?

Insecure people say "yes," when they really mean "no." Those who succeed at being themselves don't allow others to control them. They are led by their heart, not by the fear of displeasing others or being rejected by them.

We cannot get angry at people because they place demands on us. It is our responsibility to order our lives. We need to know our identity, our direction and our calling — God's will for us. We must make the decisions that will keep us pressing toward our goals. We must be focused individuals with purpose.

I can remember feeling intense pressure when people would ask me to do something that I really did not want to do. I thought they were pressuring me, but in reality it was my own fears and insecurities that were creating the pressure.

Dave is very secure, so he never feels this type of pressure. He believes he is led by the Spirit of God. If he feels led to do something, he does it. If he doesn't feel something is right for him, he doesn't do it. For him it is very simple.

I have asked him many times, "Don't you care what other people think?" His answer is also simple. He says, "What they think is not my problem." He knows his responsibility is to be what God has created him to be. He is succeeding at being himself!

Of course, there are times in life when all of us do things we would rather not do. We do things for others because we love them, and we should do that. But in doing so, we are still being led by God's Spirit to walk in love and make a sacrifice for someone else's benefit or welfare. This is entirely different from being controlled and manipulated by other people's demands and expectations.

BEING DIFFERENT IS NOT BAD ————————

The sun is glorious in one way, the moon is glorious in
another way, and the stars are glorious in their own [distinc-
tive] way; for one star differs from and surpasses another in
its beauty and brilliance.
1 Corinthians 15:41

We are all different. Like the sun, the moon and the stars, God
has created us to be different from one another, and He has done it on
purpose. Each of us meets a need, and we are all part of God's overall
plan. When we struggle to be like others, not only do we lose
ourselves, but we also grieve the Holy Spirit. God wants us to fit into
His plan, not to feel pressured trying to fit into everyone else's plans.
Different is OK; it is all right to be different.

We are all born with different temperaments, different physical
features, different fingerprints, different gifts and abilities, etc. Our
goal should be to find out what we individually are supposed to be,
and then succeed at being that.

Romans 12 teaches us that we are to give ourselves to our gift. In
other words, we are to find out what we are good at and then throw
ourselves wholeheartedly into it.

I have discovered that I enjoy doing what I am good at doing.
Some people feel they are not good at anything, but that is not true.
When we make an effort to do what others are good at doing, we
often fail because we are not gifted for those things; but that does not
mean we are good for nothing.

I tried to sew my family's clothes because my friend sewed, but I
was no good at it. I tried to learn to play guitar and sing because I
liked music and wanted to lead worship for the Bible study I was
holding in my home at the time. I could not learn to play guitar
because my fingers were too short. I seemed to sing in a key that

nobody else sang in, and I knew absolutely nothing about music theory. So I failed at that also.

To be honest, as long as I was busy trying to be everyone else, I was failing at almost everything. When I accepted what God had for me and started doing it, I began to succeed.

My pastor once told me that I was "a mouth" in the Body of Christ. We are all parts of one body, and I am a mouth. I talk! I am a teacher, a communicator; I use my voice to lead people. I have great joy since making the decision to be satisfied with myself as I am and to stop trying to be something or someone I am not. There are many things I cannot do, but I am doing what I can do.

I encourage you to focus on your potential instead of your limitations.

We all have limitations, and we must accept them. That is not bad; it is just a fact. It is wonderful to be free to be different, not to feel that something is wrong with us because we are different.

We should be free to love and accept ourselves and one another without feeling pressure to compare or compete. Secure people who know God loves them and has a plan for them are not threatened by the abilities of others. They enjoy what other people can do, and they enjoy what they can do.

In Galatians 5:26, the Apostle Paul urges us, *Let us not become vainglorious and self-conceited, competitive and challenging and provoking and irritating to one another, envying and being jealous of one another.* Then, in the next chapter, he goes on to say, *But let every person carefully scrutinize and examine and test his own conduct and his own work. He can then have the personal satisfaction and joy of doing something commendable [in itself alone] without [resorting to] boastful comparison with his neighbor* (Galatians 6:4).

Comparison and competition are worldly, not godly. The world's system demands it, but God's system condemns it.

When I stand before God, He will not ask me why I wasn't like Dave, or the Apostle Paul, or my pastor's wife, or my friend. I don't want to hear Him say to me, "Why weren't you Joyce Meyer?" I want to hear Him say, "...*Well done, good and faithful servant...*" (Matthew 25:23 KJV).

I want to be able to say to the Father what Jesus said to Him in John 17:4: *I have glorified You down here on the earth by completing the work that You gave Me to do.*

WHO IS "THEY"?

...where the Spirit of the Lord is, there is liberty.
2 Corinthians 3:17

It has occurred to me that "they" seem to run our lives. It is amazing how many decisions we make based on the opinion of "they." If we begin to listen carefully, we will realize how often we make the statement, "Well you know, they always say..."

For example, "they" decide what colors we can wear together, what clothing styles are appropriate, how we may cut our hair and what we are allowed to eat and drink. "They" happen to be a person or a group of people somewhere who are not much different from us. "They" have set a standard by doing something a certain way, and now all of us seem to feel it must be done that way, just because "they" say so.

I started realizing "they" were running my life, and I decided I didn't like it. I didn't even know who "they" were. I decided I was tired of being enslaved by what "they" wanted and that I was going to live free of the bondage of public opinion. We can all do that, because Jesus has already liberated us.

We Are Free!

So if the Son liberates you [makes you free men], then you are
really and unquestionably free.
John 8:36

Surely Jesus has set us free from being controlled and manipulated by an elusive group called "they." Surely we don't have to compare ourselves to "them" or be in competition with "them."

If we are really liberated, then we are free to be who we are — not who someone else is! That means we are free to do what God has for us to do, not what we see someone else doing.

I see many ministers struggling because they are trying to do in their ministries what they see someone else doing. A pastor may find a large church and want to know what some other pastor did to make his church grow. He may do exactly what another person did to produce excellent results, and yet for him it may not work. Why? Because what works for him is what God anoints for him, not necessarily what someone else is anointed for.

God wants us looking to Him for answers and direction, not running to and depending on other people. This does not mean that we cannot learn from each other, but we do need to stay balanced in this area.

I learned that no matter how much I may want to do what someone else is doing, I cannot do it unless God wills and anoints it for me. He might have a different plan for me. I have to accept that or I will be frustrated all my life.

"I Can Do...Whatever God Says!"

I can do all things through Christ which strengtheneth me.
Philippians 4:13 KJV

We have heard this verse quoted frequently, but I believe sometimes it is quoted out of context. It does not mean that I can do anything I want to do, or that I can do anything someone else does. It means that I can do whatever God's will is for me.

In this verse the Apostle Paul was actually referring to the ability to be abased or to abound and to be content either way. He knew that whatever state he was in, it was God's will for him at that moment, and he also knew that God would strengthen him to do what He was calling him to do.

This understanding of Philippians 4:13 has helped me a great deal in my life and ministry. It has taught me to remain within the boundaries of what the Lord has called and equipped me to do and not try to undertake things that are not within my God-given talents and abilities to accomplish. That is not negativism, it is godly wisdom.

CONTENT TO RECEIVE THE GIFT

> *John answered, A man can receive nothing [he can claim nothing, he can take unto himself nothing] except as it has been granted to him from heaven. [A man must be content to receive the gift which is given him from heaven; there is no other source].*
> *John 3:27*

This is another Scripture that has really helped me to find peace, joy and contentment in my life's work.

If you read the previous verses in John 3, you will find that some of John the Baptist's disciples were getting concerned that Jesus was baptizing too, and that everyone was leaving their master and flocking to Him. They went to John with this report. Had John not been secure in himself and in his calling, he may have become fearful and jealous. He may have felt led to compete with Jesus in order to maintain his ministry. But John's response was verse 27. His attitude was, "I can only do what I have been divinely authorized and empowered to do, so I must be content with that gift and calling."

Scriptures like these were life-changing for me. Because of my background I had many weaknesses in the area of competition. I was always comparing myself with others, jealous of them and their possessions and abilities. I wasn't being myself, I was trying to keep up with everyone else. Often I felt pressured and frustrated because I was operating outside my gifts and calling. When I finally realized that I could not do anything unless God had ordained it and anointed it, I started relaxing and saying, "I am what I am. I can't be anything unless God helps me. I am just going to concentrate on being the best me I can be."

LET GOD CHOOSE YOUR FORM OF SERVICE

I appeal to you therefore, brethren, and beg of you in view of [all] the mercies of God, to make a decisive dedication of your bodies [presenting all your members and faculties] as a living sacrifice, holy (devoted, consecrated) and well pleasing to God, which is your reasonable (rational, intelligent) service and spiritual worship.
Romans 12:1

Another thing "they" seem to decide for us is what is and what is not an important profession. We are led to believe that a doctor is more important than a factory worker, a pastor is more important than a janitor, a woman who leads a Bible study is more important than a woman who is a homemaker and mother.

If we buy into this philosophy, we will spend our lives trying to become what "they" approve of and, in the process, may very well miss our true calling in life.

One of my daughters, Sandra, is becoming quite a good public speaker. My other daughter, Laura, has one main desire, and that is to be a wife and mother. They love each other and get along great. There is no competition between them. Laura does not feel that she is "missing it," because she does not want to be in full-time ministry. She knows what she is supposed to do, and she is doing it. It is not that Sandra is "more spiritual" than Laura; they are just different, and they handle their spiritual lives two different ways.

Laura has two sons and may be raising a great world evangelist. Sometimes it is the little seemingly insignificant things in life that have the greatest impact in the end. "They" tell us that only big things are important, but God has different ideas. The thing that is important to Him is obedience. Laura is being obedient to the calling on her life, and I am just as proud of her as I am my other daughter.

I have met many pastors' wives who want to work full time in the church and be really involved in their husbands' ministries. I have met many other pastors' wives who want to be a full-time wife to their husband and the mother of his children, doing nothing in the ministry except support their husband in whatever way he may need. Often a pastor's wife suffers from insecurities and feels pressured to teach the ladies' Bible study or be involved in other aspects of her husband's ministry simply because "they" expect her to.

It seems that each role in life has expectations attached to it, but we must be sure whose expectations they are.

I remember the woman who came to the altar crying after a service. She said all her friends were attending early morning prayer at their church, and they were pressuring her to go. She did not feel led to go and was now wondering what her problem was.

"What's wrong with me, Joyce?" she asked with tears streaming down her cheeks.

I questioned her a little while and discovered that what was actually in her heart was to baby-sit the children of the ladies who were attending the morning prayer. This woman had a gift for working with children, and her desire was to help in that way.

When we pressure people to do what we are doing, or what we think they should be doing, we often miss the gift they could contribute if we would let God choose their ministry. People are naturally going to want to do what God has gifted them to do. By the same token, we won't feel fulfilled if we repress our gifts and do what others are doing just to be approved or accepted by them.

This young lady was quite relieved when I told her that absolutely nothing was wrong with her. She had a good prayer life; it just was not going to be exercised at early morning prayer at the church three times a week. I recommended that she stand her ground with her friends, telling them exactly what was on her heart. If they wanted to benefit from her gift, fine; if not, it was their loss.

I have discovered that boldness is required in order to be led by the Holy Spirit, because He may not always lead us to do what everyone else is doing. Some insecure people tend to feel "safer" doing what others do. They are fearful of "breaking the mold" or standing alone. Anytime we step outside the boundaries of what "they" say is permissible, we take a chance on being judged or criticized. Insecure people will usually give into the expectations and demands of others rather than face disapproval and possible rejection. We must not allow such things to keep us from fulfilling our God-given purpose.

HANDLING CRITICISM AND JUDGMENT

And so each of us shall give an account of himself [give an answer in reference to judgment] to God.
Romans 14:12

Confronting the criticism and judgment of other people becomes easier when we remember that ultimately it is before our own Master that we stand or fall. (Romans 14:4.) In the end we will answer to God alone. It is a sin to be critical and judgmental, but it is equally sinful to permit the adverse opinions of other people to control our decisions. Romans 14:23 KJV says that whatever is not of faith is sin.

We crave acceptance; therefore, criticism and judgment are hard on us mentally and emotionally. The fact is, it hurts to be criticized or judged! However, if we are to succeed at being ourselves, we must have the same attitude that Paul displayed when he wrote:

> *But [as for me personally] it matters very little to me that I should be put on trial by you [on this point], and that you or any other human tribunal should investigate and question and cross-question me. I do not even put myself on trial and judge myself.*
>
> *I am not conscious of anything against myself, and I feel blameless; but I am not vindicated and acquitted before God on that account. It is the Lord [Himself] Who examines and judges me.*
> *1 Corinthians 4:3,4*

I particularly enjoy the Ben Campbell Johnson paraphrase of this passage:

> *I am not the least concerned with the fact that you are deciding what is right and what is wrong with me...and even passing sentence on me. Neither you nor anyone else can put me down unless I first put myself down. (And I'm not doing that.) But though I don't know of anything against me, my ignorance doesn't mean I am correct in my appraisal because the final evaluation is in God's hands.*

Criticism and judgment are the devil's tools. He uses them to stop people from fulfilling their destiny and to steal their liberty and creativity.

Some people criticize whatever is different from their choices. It is interesting to note that most of these people are also very insecure —

that is why they are uncomfortable with people who don't conform to their way of thinking or acting.

When I was still in my insecure years I found myself being judgmental most of the time, and, of course, always toward those who didn't think or act as I did. They made me uncomfortable. I finally realized that their decision to be different challenged my decision.

Secure people can handle being the only ones doing something. They can easily allow friends and family members the liberty to make their own choices.

As I mentioned previously, my husband Dave is very secure, and he has allowed me to succeed at being me. He is not threatened by my success in life because he is comfortable with himself. He likes who he is. There is no competition between us. Neither of us is more important than the other. We are simply free to be all we can be, and yet we are very different.

We don't judge and criticize each other's differences, we just accept them. It wasn't always that way, but we learned over the years that we are called to love one another, not change one another.

Paul did not allow the opinions of others to change his destiny. In Galatians 1:10 he said if he had been seeking popularity with people, he would not have become an apostle of the Lord Jesus Christ. This statement should teach us a lot. How can we succeed at being ourselves if we are overly concerned about what other people think?

In Philippians 2:7 KJV Paul tells us that Jesus ...*made himself of no reputation....* Jesus obviously wasn't concerned about what others thought. He had a goal — to do the Father's will — no more, no less. He knew He had to maintain His freedom in order to fulfill His destiny.

Criticism and judgment may be painful but not as painful as allowing ourselves to be controlled and manipulated by that criticism and judgment. To me, the greatest tragedy in life would be to get old and feel that somewhere along the way I had lost myself and never succeeded at being me.

Have you lost yourself, or have you found yourself?

5

CONFIDENCE
IS REQUIRED

5
CONFIDENCE
IS REQUIRED

To succeed at being ourselves, we must be confident. It is not self-confidence we are to seek, but confidence in Christ. I like *The Amplified Bible* translation of Philippians 4:13 which says in part, *[...I am self-sufficient in Christ's sufficiency]*. It is actually a sin to be confident in ourselves — but to be confident in Christ should be the goal of every believer.

[Most] blessed is the man who believes in, trusts in, and relies on the Lord, and whose hope and confidence the Lord is.
JEREMIAH 17:7

Jesus said, *...apart from Me [cut off from vital union with Me] you can do nothing* (John 15:5). It seems to take us forever to really learn this truth. We keep attempting to do things in the strength of our own flesh, instead of placing all our confidence in Him.

Most of our internal agony, our struggling and frustration, come from misplaced confidence. In Philippians 3:3 Paul says that we are to put no confidence in the flesh. This means our own selves as well as our friends and family. I am not saying that we cannot trust anyone, but if we give to others or to ourselves the trust that belongs to God alone, we will not experience victory. God will not allow us to succeed until our confidence is in the right place, or more correctly, in the right Person. He is willing to give us the victory, but He must have the glory, which is the credit that is due Him.

HAVE CONFIDENCE IN GOD ALONE

Thus says the Lord: Cursed [with great evil] is the strong man who trusts in and relies on frail man, making weak [human] flesh his arm, and whose mind and heart turn aside from the Lord.
Jeremiah 17:5

In order to succeed at anything, we must have confidence, but first and foremost it must be confidence in God, not confidence in anything else. We must develop confidence in God's love, goodness and mercy. We must believe that He wants us to succeed.

God did not create us for failure. We may fail at some things on our way to success, but if we trust Him, He will take even our mistakes and work them out for our good. (Romans 8:28.)

Hebrews 3:6 tells us we must ...*hold fast and firm to the end our joyful and exultant confidence and sense of triumph in our hope [in Christ].* It is important to realize that a mistake is not the end of things, if we hold on to our confidence.

I have discovered that God will take my mistakes and turn them into miracles, if I continue to trust confidently in Him.

We all have a destiny, and in my case I was destined to become a Bible teacher and minister. It was God's will for me from before the foundation of the earth that I should give birth to and operate a ministry called Life In The Word. If I had not done this, I would never have succeeded at being myself. I would have felt frustrated and unfulfilled all of my life.

Just because we are destined to do something does not mean that it will automatically happen. I went through many things while God was developing me and my ministry. Many times I felt like giving up and quitting. Often I lost my confidence concerning the call on my life. Each time I had to get my confidence back before I could go forward again. Confidence is definitely required for any of us to truly succeed at being ourselves.

BE CONSISTENTLY CONFIDENT

> ...*The man who through faith is just and upright...shall live by faith.*
> *Romans 1:17*

Confidence is actually faith in God. We must learn to be consistently confident, not occasionally confident.

For example, I had to learn to remain confident in God when someone got up and walked out while I was preaching. In the beginning of my ministry that type of occurrence brought out all of my insecurities and practically destroyed my confidence.

I had been told by friends and family that a woman should not be preaching the Word of God. I also knew that some people, particularly some men, had difficulty receiving the Word from a woman. It was confusing to me because I knew God had called me and anointed me to preach His Word. I could not have done it otherwise, but I was still affected by the rejection of people, because I was lacking in confidence. I had to grow in confidence to the place where people's opinions and their acceptance or rejection did not alter my confidence level. My confidence had to be in God, not in people.

When the growth and progress of my ministry seemed to be painfully slow, I had to practice being consistently confident. It is easier to remain confident when we see progress, but during a time of waiting the devil attacks our confidence and attempts to destroy it.

Basically, Romans 1:17 tells us that we can go from faith to faith. I spent many years going from faith to doubt to unbelief and then back to faith. I lost a lot of precious time until I became consistent in my faith walk. Since then, I have tried to practice being confident in all things. I have learned that when I lose my confidence, I leave a door open for the devil.

During those times when Satan attacked my confidence level while I was ministering the Word, I began to realize that if I did not quickly stand against those attacks, things would go from bad to worse. I learned that once I gave the devil a foothold, he often got a stronghold. If I allowed him to steal my confidence, I suddenly had no faith for anything I was doing in the services.

I would become fearful about the offering. I would think, "What if people are offended because I am talking about money?" I would become fearful about advertising my teaching tapes. I would think, "People don't like me talking about these tapes!" While I was teaching the Word I would think all kinds of negative thoughts that provoked fear in me, things like, "This message makes no sense. I'm boring everyone. This is not the right message for tonight; I should have preached something else."

During those demonic attacks, which gained entrance through my lack of confidence, if anyone did get up and leave, I was certain it was because of me.

I recall an instance that occurred in Oklahoma City. A woman who was sitting in the second row got up and left about five minutes after I had begun my message. I immediately felt insecure, and Satan started shaking my confidence. I was bothered throughout the entire service. I commented to Dave about it later that evening, and he said, "Oh, I forgot to tell you, that woman said she had to go to work, but she loves you so much and gets so much out of your teaching she decided if she could only be there for the worship and even five minutes of your teaching, it was worth it to her to come."

We can readily see from this instance how Satan works to deceive us. If my confidence level had been consistent and strong, I would have thought positively instead of negatively in that situation.

God has told me that above all else I must be consistently confident. When I lose my confidence, I give place to the devil.

The same principle applies to you.

Be confident about your gifts and calling, your ability in Christ. Believe you hear from God and that you are led by the Holy Spirit. Be confident that people like you, and you will discover that more people do. Be bold in the Lord. See yourself as a winner in Him!

MORE THAN CONQUERORS

> *Yet amid all these things we are more than conquerors and gain a surpassing victory through Him Who loved us.*
> Romans 8:37

We need to have a sense of triumph. In Romans 8:37 Paul assures us that through Christ Jesus we are more than conquerors. Believing that truth gives us confidence.

I once heard that a woman is more than a conqueror if her husband goes out, works all week and brings his paycheck home to her. But God spoke to me and said, "You're more than a conqueror when you know that you already have the victory before you ever get a problem."

Sometimes our confidence is shaken when trials come, especially if they are lengthy. We should have so much confidence in God's love for us that no matter what comes against us, we know deep inside that we are more than conquerors. If we are truly confident, we have no need to fear trouble, challenges or trying times, because we know they will pass.

Whenever a trial of any kind comes against you, always remember: *This too shall pass!* Be confident that during the trial you will learn something that will help you in the future.

Without confidence we are stifled at every turn. Satan drops a bomb, and our dreams are destroyed. Eventually we start over, but we never make much progress. We start and get defeated, start and get defeated, start and get defeated, over and over again.

But those who are consistently confident, those who know they are more than conquerors through Jesus Christ, make rapid progress.

We must take a step of faith and decide to be confident in all things. God may have to correct us occasionally, but that is better than playing it safe and never doing anything. Confident people get the job done, they have the ministries that are making a difference in the world today. They are fulfilled because they are succeeding at being themselves.

God has dealt with me about confidence. He once said to me, "Joyce, be confident in your prayer life, be confident that you hear from Me. Be confident that you are walking in My will. Be confident that you are preaching the right message. Be confident when you speak a word in season to someone who needs to hear it." He continues to press upon me the importance of being confident in Him.

I am now impressing upon you the importance of being confident. Make a decision that self-doubt is a thing of the past.

THE TORMENT OF SELF-DOUBT

> David was greatly distressed, for the men spoke of stoning him because the souls of them all were bitterly grieved, each man for his sons and daughters. But David encouraged and strengthened himself in the Lord his God.
> 1 Samuel 30:6

If we don't believe in ourselves, who is going to? God believes in us, and it is a good thing too; otherwise, we might never make any progress. In our lives, we cannot wait for someone else to come along and encourage us to be all we can be. We may be blessed enough to have that kind of support, but we may not.

When David and his men found themselves in a seemingly hopeless situation, which the men blamed on him, David encouraged and strengthened himself in the Lord. Later on, that situation was totally turned around. (1 Samuel 30:1-20.)

On an earlier occasion, when David was just a boy, everyone around him was discouraging him concerning his ability to fight against Goliath. They told him he was too young and too inexperienced, he didn't have the right armor or the right weapons, the giant was too big and too powerful, and on and on. David, however, was confident in God.

Actually all of the things people said were true. David was young, inexperienced, without natural armor or weapons, and Goliath was definitely bigger and more powerful than he was. But David knew his God and had confidence in Him. He believed that God would be strong in his weakness and give him the victory. He went out in the name of the Lord, with a heart full of confidence, and became a giant-killer who was eventually crowned king. (1 Samuel 17.)

David had no one to believe in him, so he believed in himself. He believed in God's ability in him.

The Lord told me once that if I didn't believe in myself, I really did not believe in Him properly. He said, "I am in you, but I can only do through you what you believe."

Self-doubt is absolutely tormenting. I lived in it for many years, and I personally prefer confidence.

You may be thinking, "Well, Joyce, I wish I had confidence."

Confidence is something we decide to have. We learn about God — about His love, His ways and His Word — then ultimately we must *decide* whether we believe or not. If we do believe, then we have confidence. If we don't believe, we live in doubt about everything.

Self-doubt makes us double-minded, and James 1:8 KJV teaches us that *a double minded man is unstable in all his ways.* He really cannot go forward until he decides to believe in God and in himself.

STOP SELLING YOURSELF SHORT! ————————————

> *Now thanks be to God who always leads us in triumph in*
> *Christ....*
> *2 Corinthians 2:14 NKJV*

I encourage you to take a big step of faith and *stop doubting yourself.* As the old saying goes, "Don't sell yourself short." You have more capabilities than you think you do. You are able to do a lot more than you have ever done in the past. God will help you, if you will put your trust in Him and stop doubting yourself.

Like everyone else, you will make mistakes — but God will allow you to learn from them and will actually work them out to your good if you will decide not to be defeated by them. When doubt begins to torment your mind, start speaking the Word of God out of your mouth, and you will win the battle.

6

FREE TO DEVELOP YOUR POTENTIAL

6
FREE TO DEVELOP YOUR POTENTIAL

When we are confident and free from tormenting fears, we are able to develop our potential and succeed at being all God intended us to be. But we cannot develop our potential if we fear failure. We will be so afraid of failing or making mistakes that it will prevent us from stepping out.

Do you not know that in a race all the runners compete, but [only] one receives the prize? So run [your race] that you may lay hold [of the prize] and make it yours.
1 CORINTHIANS 9:24

I recently spoke to a young man on our staff who has great potential and yet he had turned down two promotions we offered him. I felt in my spirit that he was insecure and unaware of how much he could accomplish for the Kingdom of God if he would only step out in faith and confidence. His insecurities had him trapped. He was doing his current job excellently and receiving good comments from everyone about it, but he was afraid to accept promotion. It was easier and more comfortable to just remain in the same position.

When we are insecure, frequently we will stay with what is safe and familiar rather than taking a chance on stepping out and failing.

I felt that because of this young man's particular personality type, he did not like change. His hesitancy to accept greater responsibility was causing him to turn down opportunities to advance. He said he felt that he just was not ready, and the truth is that none of us is ever ready. But when God is ready to move in our lives, we need to believe that He will equip us with what we need at the time we need it.

Our problem is not honestly feeling we are not ready for the next step, it is pridefully feeling we are ready when we really aren't. Pride always causes problems and ultimate failure. Humbly leaning on God leads to success. I believe God calls us to step out when we *don't* feel ready so we will have to lean on Him totally.

I talked with the young man and encouraged him. He said that he knew I was right and that he wanted to start stepping out. He said he had been asking God to let him do something different, and yet every time he was offered some new opportunity for growth and service, he always turned it down.

Insecurity, self-doubt and fear can totally prevent us from ever reaching our full potential. But if our confidence is in Christ rather than in ourselves, we are free to develop our potential, because we are free from the fear of failure.

As Christians, our #1 job is the development of personal potential. Noah Webster's 1828 *American Dictionary of the English Language* defines *potential* in part as "existing in possibility, not in act."[1] It then defines *potentiality* in part as "not positively."[2]

In other words, where there is potential, all the parts necessary for success are there, but they are not yet put into action. They still need something to propel them, something to empower and motivate them. They are often in embryonic form—they need to be developed.

Potential cannot manifest without form. There must be something for it to be poured into, something that will cause it to take shape and become useful. When we offered that young man a promotion, we were offering him a form in which to pour his potential. He would never see it take shape unless he did something to exercise it. He had potential, but it needed to be developed.

A developer of a subdivision has plans in his office, but they remain only drawings on paper until they are actually manifested as houses. What stands in the space between potential and manifestation? I believe it is three things: time, determination and hard work!

The amount of undeveloped, wasted potential in the world is pathetic. God places a part of Himself in each of us. We are created in His image, and He is filled with potential — *with God nothing is impossible.* (Matthew 19:26, author's paraphrase.)

All of us have potential and many of us want a manifestation of it, but too often we are not willing to wait, be determined and work hard at developing that potential. We have a lot of "wish bone," but not much "back bone."

The development and manifestation of potential requires firm faith, not wishful thinking.

Dreams and visions develop in a way similar to the way a child develops in the womb of its mother. Certain things must be done certain ways or the pregnant woman will never deliver a healthy baby. She must wait full term; a premature birth will produce a sickly child. She must also be fully determined and willing to work hard to bring forth that which is within her. Any woman who has ever given birth and remembers her labor can say yes and amen to that fact.

DON'T MAKE SMALL PLANS!

> *Any enterprise is built by wise planning, becomes strong through common sense, and profits wonderfully by keeping abreast of the facts.*
> *Proverbs 24:3,4 TLB*

I hope you have a dream or a vision in your heart for something greater than what you have now. Ephesians 3:20 KJV tells us that God is able to do exceedingly abundantly above and beyond all that we can hope or ask or think. If we are not thinking, hoping or asking for anything, we are cheating ourselves. We need to think big thoughts, hope for big things and ask for big things.

I always say, I would rather ask God for a lot and get half of it, than to ask Him for a little and get all of it. However, it is an unwise person who only thinks, dreams and asks big but fails to realize that an enterprise is built by wise planning.

Dreams for the future are possibilities, but not what I call "positivelies." In other words, they are possible, but they will not positively occur unless we do our part.

When we see a twenty-year-old athlete who is a gold medalist in the Olympics, we know that he spent many years practicing while others were playing games. He may not have had all the "fun" his friends had, but he did develop his potential. Now he has something that will bring him joy for the rest of his life.

Far too many people take the "quick fix" method for everything. They only want what makes them feel good right now. They are not willing to invest for the future.

Don't just enter the race for the fun of being in it — *run to win!* (1 Corinthians 9:24,25.)

There is a gold mine hidden in every life, but we have to dig to get to it. We must be willing to dig deep and go beyond how we feel or what is convenient. If we will dig down deep into the spirit, we will find strength we never knew we had.

When God called me into the ministry, I wanted to fulfill His call more than anything. I didn't even know where to begin, let alone how to finish the task. As God gave me anointed ideas and opened to me doors of opportunity for service, I stepped out in faith. Each time He met me with the strength, wisdom and ability that was needed to be successful. I had reserves that I didn't even know existed, but God already knew what He had placed in me long ago.

Quite often we look at a task and think there is no way we can do what needs to be done. That happens because we look at ourselves when we should be looking at God.

When the Lord called Joshua to take the place of Moses and lead the Israelites into the Promised Land, He said to him, ...*As I was with Moses, so I will be with you; I will not fail you or forsake you* (Joshua 1:5).

If God promises to be with us — and He does — that is really all we need. His strength is made perfect in our weakness. (2 Corinthians 12:9 KJV.) Whatever ingredients we are lacking in the natural man, He adds to the spiritual man. We can draw what we need out of the spirit.

DRAW UPON THE STRENGTH OF THE LORD

> *...be strong in the Lord [be empowered through your union with Him]; draw your strength from Him [that strength which His boundless might provides].*
> *Ephesians 6:10*

In this passage, Paul assures us that the Holy Spirit will pour strength into our human spirit as we fellowship with Him.

Then in Ephesians 3:16 Paul prays to the Lord for us, *May He grant you out of the rich treasury of His glory to be strengthened and reinforced with mighty power in the inner man by the [Holy] Spirit [Himself indwelling your innermost being and personality].*

In Isaiah 40:31 KJV the prophet tells us that ...*they that wait upon the Lord shall renew their strength; they shall mount up with wings as eagles; they shall run, and not be weary; and they shall walk, and not faint.*

It is very obvious from these Scriptures and others like them that we are strengthened as we go to God for what we are lacking.

When I first started out in the ministry, I had potential, but I had to work with what I had for a long time. God helped me, and little by little I advanced toward the place I am today. It certainly was not always easy. There were many, many times when I thought I just could not go on. The responsibility often seemed more than I could handle. After all, I am also a wife and the mother of four wonderful children. But I was motivated by the desire to be all I could be.

In my life there had been many people who had told me that I would never amount to anything, so I was determined not to succumb to their negative prophecies. God had told me that I had potential and a future and that if I would trust Him, work hard and refuse to give up, He would walk me across the finish line.

Most of the things that are truly worth doing are never easy — we are not filled with the Spirit of God to do easy things. He fills us with His Spirit so we can do impossible things!

If you want to develop your potential and succeed at being all you can be, *keep your eyes on the prize and press on!* It won't all be easy, but it will all be worthwhile.

I cannot begin to tell you how glad I am now that I did not give up somewhere along the way. It would have been easy to make excuses and quit, but I would be sitting somewhere now totally unfulfilled and unhappy, probably wondering why life had treated me so badly.

Most of those who blame everyone and everything for their failures had potential but either did not know how to develop it or were unwilling to meet its requirements.

When things don't work out in our lives, it is not God's fault. He has a great plan for each one of us. It isn't really circumstances that are to blame, because they can be overcome with faith and determination. It isn't other people who are the problem because Romans 8:31 says, *...If God is for us, who [can be] against us?...* Even though people do come against us, and Satan does use them to hinder and torment us, they cannot prevail. If God is on our side, it just does not matter who comes against us; they are not mightier than He is.

The truth is, when things don't work out for us, and we feel that we are sitting on the sidelines somewhere with life passing us by while everyone else is successful, it is because we have not obeyed God, not pressed on and been willing to take giant steps of faith. We have not been willing to look foolish, to be judged and criticized, to be laughed at, to be rejected and labeled radicals who need to calm down and just "go with the flow."

The world wants us to *conform*, but the Lord wants to *transform* us, if we will do things His way. He will take us and change us into something more than we could have ever dreamed — if we will refuse to give up and just keep running the race that is set before us.

RUNNING THE RACE

> *...let us strip off and throw aside every encumbrance (unnecessary weight) and that sin which so readily (deftly and cleverly) clings to and entangles us, and let us run with patient endurance and steady and active persistence the appointed course of the race that is set before us.*
> *Hebrews 12:1*

When the writer of the letter to the Hebrews told them to *strip off and throw aside every encumbrance*, he was thinking of the runners in his day who entered races with the intention of winning. They literally stripped off their clothes down to a simple loincloth. They made sure there was nothing that could entangle them and prevent them from running their fastest. They were running to win! Some people run, but not to win — they just want the fun of being in the race.

To develop our potential and succeed at becoming what God intended us to be, we will have to lay aside other things. To be a winner in life we must do those things that support our goals and help us fulfill our purpose. We must learn to say "no" to well-meaning people who want us to get involved in endless things that ultimately steal our time and produce no fruit.

The Apostle Paul was intent on developing his potential. He pictured himself in a race, straining every nerve and muscle and exerting every ounce of strength, like a runner, with bulging veins, lest he come short of the goal.

We must make up our mind and get into agreement with God that we are going to be excellent, not mediocre. We must take an inventory of our life and prune off anything in it that entangles us or simply steals our time. We must be determined, work hard, and refuse to quit or give up — drawing strength from God and not depending on ourselves. If we will do these things persistently, we will eventually have victory. If we are in the race just to have fun, we will not win the prize.

Hebrews 12:1 tells us to strip off and throw aside every encumbrance and the *sin* which entangles us. It is virtually impossible to be a spiritual success with known, willful sin in our lives. I don't mean to say that we must be 100 percent perfect in order for God to use us, but I am saying that we must have an aggressive attitude about keeping sin out of our lives. When God says something is wrong, then it is wrong. We don't need to discuss, theorize, blame, make excuses or feel sorry for ourselves — we need to agree with God, ask for forgiveness and work with the Holy Spirit to get that thing out of our lives forever.

I fear that the modern-day Church is not concerned nearly enough about holiness. People don't usually get excited when we preach about it, and I have noticed they don't buy many teaching albums on the subject. A new tape series on success is a good seller, but holiness and the crucifixion of the flesh are not as popular, at least not with some people. But thank God, there is the remnant, those few rare individuals who are not just out for "fun" but who intend to glorify God with their lives by being all He intended them to be.

BE TEMPERATE IN ALL THINGS ————————————

*Do you not know that in a race all the runners compete, but
[only] one receives the prize? So run [your race] that you may
lay hold [of the prize] and make it yours.*

*Now every athlete who goes into training conducts himself
temperately and restricts himself in all things. They do it to
win a wreath that will soon wither, but we [do it to receive a
crown of eternal blessedness] that cannot wither.*

*Therefore I do not run uncertainly (without definite aim).
I do not box like one beating the air and striking without
an adversary.*

*But [like a boxer] I buffet my body [handle it roughly, disci-
pline it by hardships] and subdue it, for fear that after
proclaiming to others the Gospel and things pertaining to it, I
myself should become unfit [not stand the test, be unapproved
and rejected as a counterfeit].*

1 Corinthians 9:24-27

Those of us who intend to run the race to win must conduct
ourselves temperately and restrict ourselves in all things. We cannot
expect someone else to make us do what is right. We must listen to
the Holy Spirit and take action ourselves.

Paul said he buffeted his body. He meant that he disciplined it
because he did not want to preach to others, telling them what they
should do, and then fail to do it himself. Paul was running the race to
win! He knew he could not develop his potential without bringing his
body, mind and emotions under the control of his spirit.

Self-discipline is the most important feature in any life, but especially
in the life of the Christian. Unless we discipline our minds, our mouths
and our emotions, we will live in ruin. Unless we learn to rule our temper,
we can never achieve the success that rightfully belongs to us.

Consider the following Scriptures:

> *He who foams up quickly and flies into a **passion** deals foolishly....*
> *Proverbs 14:17*

> *He who is slow to anger is better than the mighty, he who*
> *rules his [own] spirit than he who takes a city.*
> *Proverbs 16:32*

> *Do not be quick in spirit to be angry or vexed, for anger and*
> *vexation lodge in the bosom of fools.*
> *Ecclesiastes 7:9*

> *...Let every man be...slow...to get angry.*
> *For man's anger does not promote the righteousness God*
> *[wishes and requires].*
> *James 1:19,20*

The statement that man's anger does not promote the righteousness God wishes or requires means that anger is not the right way for man to behave; it will not bring the right thing into his life.

Part of the righteousness God wishes and desires for us is the development of personal potential. Angry people are too busy being angry ever to succeed at being the best they can be.

If we are truly intent on running the race to win, we must resist negative emotions. There are a great many negative emotions other than just anger, and we certainly should know what they are and be ready to take authority and control over them as soon as they rear their ugly heads. The following is a partial list of negative emotions we must watch out for:

anger

bitterness

depression

despair

discouragement

envy

greed

hate

impatience

jealousy

laziness

lust

offense

pride

resentment

sadness

self-pity

unforgiveness

"LET US RUN WITH PATIENCE"

> *...let us run with patience the race that is set before us.*
> *Hebrews 12:1 KJV*

The *King James Version* of Hebrews 12:1 not only encourages us to run the race, but also to run it with patience. We cannot come to fullness without patience. To illustrate, here is a story based on articles that appeared in the *Houston Chronicle* in 1997:

"Jell-O turns 100 this year and the story surrounding its inventor is truly ironic. In 1897, Pearl Wait wore several hats. He was a construction worker who dabbled in patent medicines and sold his ailment remedies door-to-door. In the midst of his tinkering he hit upon the idea of mixing fruit flavoring with granulated gelatin. His wife named it 'Jell-O' and Wait had one more product to peddle. Unfortunately, sales weren't as strong as he'd hoped, so in 1899, Pearl Wait sold his Jell-O rights to Orator Woodward for $450. Woodward knew the value of marketing so within just eight brief years, Wait's neighbor turned a $450 investment into a $1 million business. Today, not a single relative of Pearl Wait receives royalties from the 1.1 million boxes of Jell-O that are sold each day. Why? Because Wait just couldn't wait!"[3]

This impatient attitude is one of the main reasons that many people never reach their full potential. You may remember that earlier I said time is one of the things that must come between potential and desired manifestation. Pearl Wait desired the manifestation of becoming rich from his invention of Jell-O, but his impatience prevented him from enjoying the full potential of it.

PATIENCE WORKS PERFECTION

> *My brethren, count it all joy when you fall into various trials,*
> *knowing that the testing of your faith produces patience.*
> *But let patience have its perfect work, that you may be perfect*
> *and complete, lacking nothing.*
> *James 1:2–4 NKJV*

This passage tells us that when patience has had its perfect work, we will be perfect (fully developed) and complete, lacking nothing. It also speaks about trials of all kinds, and it is during these trials that we are instructed to be patient.

As I noted in my book, *Battlefield of the Mind*, "Patience is not the ability to wait, it is the ability to keep a good attitude while waiting."[4]

Patience is a fruit of the Spirit that manifests in a calm, positive attitude. Impatience is filled with negative emotions and is one of Satan's tools used to prevent us from reaching fullness and completeness.

Hebrews 10:36 lets us know that we need patience so that we *...may perform and **fully** accomplish the will of God....*

I asked the Lord, "When, God, when?" thousands of times before I finally realized that according to Psalm 31:15 my times are in His hands. God knows the exact time that is right for everything, and none of our impatience is going to rush Him.

WAIT ON GOD'S PERFECT TIMING

And let us not be weary in well doing: for in due season we shall reap, if we faint not.
Galatians 6:9 KJV

"Due season" is God's season, not ours. We are in a hurry, God isn't. He takes time to do things right — He lays a solid foundation before He attempts to build a building. We are God's building under construction. He is the Master Builder, and He knows what He is doing. We may not know what He is doing, but He does, and that will have to be good enough. We may not always know, but we can be satisfied to know the One Who knows.

God's timing seems to be His own little secret. The Bible promises us that He will never be late, but I have also discovered that He is usually not early. It seems that He takes every available opportunity to develop the fruit of patience in us.

Vine's dictionary of Greek words begins the definition of *patience* (in James 1:3), as "Patience, which grows only in trial...."[5] Patience is a fruit of the Spirit that grows under trial.

My own particular natural temperament is filled with impatience. I have become much more patient over the years, but all the waiting required to teach me patience was hard on me. I wanted everything *now!*

I finally found out that we can fall on the Rock (Jesus) and be broken, or the Rock will fall on us and break us! (Matthew 21:44.) In other words, we can cooperate with the Holy Spirit and not resist the work of God He is doing in us, or we can refuse to cooperate willingly, and in due time God will have to deal with us more harshly than He might desire. Things will still ultimately work out for our good, but it is always better to give something up than to have it taken away.

I needed to surrender my will to the will of God. I needed to place myself in His hands and trust His timing. It sounds easy, but it wasn't, at least not for me.

I am grateful that our natural temperaments can become "Spirit-controlled temperaments." The fruit of the Spirit is in us and is being developed along with everything else. As our potential is developed, so is our character, along with a Christlike attitude. It all moves along together. There are several things that must arrive at the finish line at the same time in order for us to win the race.

Developed potential without character does not glorify God. If we were to become a huge success and yet be harsh with people — that would not be pleasing to the Lord. Therefore, if we get ahead of ourselves in one area, He gently but firmly blocks our progress in that area until the other ones catch up.

When my ministry growth started getting ahead of my spiritual growth, God graciously blocked the progress of the ministry growth. Of course, I did not understand and was quite put out. I spent my time rebuking demons and trying to do what I thought was spiritual warfare. I was sure that Satan was opposing me — I discovered it was

God. I was ahead of Him, and He was putting on the brakes whether I liked it or not.

We don't appreciate any of this while it is happening, but later on we realize what an awful mess we would have made if things had been done on our timetable instead of on God's.

Patience is vital to the development of our full potential. Actually our potential is only developed as our patience is developed. It is God's way — there is no other, so why not settle down and enjoy the journey!

If we don't develop our potential, it won't get developed because no one else is interested in doing it for us. Occasionally we do find those rare individuals who delight in helping others be all they can be — but they are rare! My husband Dave has done that for me, and I am very grateful to him for helping me be all I can be. I am succeeding at being myself, and I want the same thing for you.

Find out what you want to do and begin to train yourself for it. Be relentless in your pursuit of reaching your full potential.

If you know you can write great songs, then develop your gift; arrange your life so you can write songs. If you know you can lead worship, then practice, learn music, sing with all your mind and heart and believe. Begin leading worship, even if you start with only you and the cat, or you and your children. If you know you have a talent for business, an ability to make money, then study, pray, go to school, step out.

Whatever your gift and calling, entrust it to the Lord and begin to *develop your potential.*

In some way we should improve ourselves every day. We should go forward, letting go of what lies behind. That includes past mistakes and past victories. Even hanging onto the glory of past victories can prevent us from being all God wants us to be in the future.

Make a decision right now that you will *never be satisfied with being anything less than all you can be.*

7

KNOW THE DIFFERENCE
BETWEEN YOUR
"WHO" AND YOUR "DO"

7
KNOW THE DIFFERENCE BETWEEN YOUR "WHO" AND YOUR "DO"

If we truly desire to *succeed at being ourselves,* it is absolutely necessary that we have a thorough understanding of what justifies us and makes us right with God. As we have seen in Ephesians 2:8,9, we are justified by faith in Christ alone and not by our works.

For we hold that a man is justified and made upright by faith independent of and distinctly apart from good deeds (works of the Law). [The observance of the Law has nothing to do with justification.]
ROMANS 3:28

If we have *real faith,* we will do good works, but our dependence will not be on works. Our works will be done as an act of love for God — in obedience to Him — rather than as a "work of the flesh" by which we hope to gain right standing and acceptance with Him.

Most people in our society spend a large majority of their lives, and perhaps even their entire lives, feeling wrong about themselves. The world, it seems, continually gives us the message that our worth and value are connected to our "doing." We say things to one another like: "How are you *doing?*" "What are you *doing?*" and "What do you *do* for a living?" Satan wants us to be more interested in what we do than in who we are as individuals. This type of mindset is deeply rooted in our thinking patterns and is not easily pulled out.

While we were growing up, our family members compared our performance with the performance of others, and we were questioned regarding why we were not doing as well as our cousin, the child next door or one of our siblings. We felt we were doing the best we could and had no answer to the demanding questions, but we determined that we would *try harder.* And we did. We tried and tried and tried, and it all seemed to no avail. No matter how hard we tried, it seemed that someone was still not satisfied. We were still getting the message that something was wrong with us. We thought if we could do something great, then we would be accepted by God and others.

This theory only leaves people worn out, burned out, confused and in some cases mentally ill. I definitely believe that not knowing who they are is what drives millions of people to therapists, counselors, psychiatrists and psychologists. They want someone to talk to who will understand them, someone who won't make them feel guilty. They have not been affirmed by their parents or their peers, and as a result they feel deeply flawed. They think they have some kind of mental, social or psychological problem, when really all they need is unconditional love and acceptance.

You and I may have wrong behavior, but it will not be changed until we are accepted and loved apart from what we do.

Jesus offers the world what it is looking for, but Satan has kept the secret well hidden. The Church in many instances has magnified rules and regulations instead of personal relationship with the Father through Jesus Christ the Son.

SOMEONE WHO UNDERSTANDS

> *For we do not have a High Priest Who is unable to understand and sympathize and have a shared feeling with our weaknesses and infirmities and liability to the assaults of temptation, but One Who has been tempted in every respect as we are, yet without sinning.*
> *Let us then fearlessly and confidently and boldly draw near to the throne of grace (the throne of God's unmerited favor to us sinners), that we may receive mercy [for our failures] and find grace to help in good time for every need [appropriate help and well-timed help, coming just when we need it].*
> *Hebrews 4:15,16*

There are several key words in these two verses that should not be missed: understand, grace, favor, receive and mercy. These are all "giving words," that is, words that represent God's giving to us what we do not deserve, simply because He is so good. Of these words, one of the most important is *understand*.

From this one passage we see that Jesus understands us.

I cannot begin to tell you how comforting it was to me to learn that *Jesus understands me!*

Jesus understands us when nobody else does. He even understands us when we don't understand ourselves. He knows "the why behind the what." Let me explain what I mean by that statement.

People only see what we do, and they want to know why we are not doing it better, or why we are doing it at all. Jesus knows why we behave the way we do. He sees and remembers all the emotional wounds and bruises in our past. He knows what we were created for. He knows the temperament that was given to us in our mother's womb. He knows and understands our weaknesses (which all of us have). He knows about every fear, every insecurity, every doubt, all our wrong thinking about ourselves.

Once we enter into personal relationship with Him by being born again (accepting Him as Savior and Lord), He begins a process of restoration in our lives that will not be entirely finished until we leave the earth. One by one He restores to us everything Satan has stolen from us.

We must aggressively resist the legalistic attitudes that are prevalent in our society. Legalism involves "doing"; it is not about "being."

We must understand the difference between our "who" and our "do."

Jesus understands us, He loves us unconditionally and He is committed to working with us through the Holy Spirit — and He does not condemn us while He is at it.

The world demands that we change. It persistently gives us the message that something is wrong with us if we cannot do what is expected of us. On our own, we will never be able to do all that is expected of us. Our only hope is in who we are Christ.

"IN CHRIST"

> For *in Him* we live and move and have our being....
> Acts 17:28

The phrases "in Christ," "in Him" or "in Whom," which are found throughout many books of the New Testament, are vitally important. If they are not understood, we will never have proper insight concerning our "who" and will be frustrated as we spend our lives trying to improve our "do."

When we receive Jesus Christ as Savior, we are considered to be "in Him." What He earned and deserves we get by inheritance. Looking at our relationship with our natural children may help impart understanding on this subject.

I have four children who were originally "in me." Now much of their looks and personalities result from the fact that they began their lives "in me." They received of my physical makeup, my nature, my temperament and so forth. Now that they are grown, they are free to go about life "doing" things that will make me proud of them — but, it must never be forgotten that they began "in me." That relationship will last forever.

Relationship with Jesus is referred to in John 3:3 as being "born again." Nicodemus asked Jesus, "How can a man enter his mother's womb again?" (v. 4.) He was failing to see that Jesus was speaking of a spiritual birth, a birth by which we are taken out of a worldly way of living and placed "into Christ" and a new way of thinking, speaking and acting.

We must know who we are in Christ. It is our beginning, the place from which we begin the new life. Without a deep understanding of this truth, we will ramble around in life and even in Christianity believing the lie that our acceptance by God is based on our performance.

The truth is, our acceptance by God is based on Jesus' performance, not ours. When He died on the cross, we died with Him. When He was buried, we were buried with Him. When He was resurrected, we were resurrected with Him. That is the way God chooses to see all of us who sincerely believe in Jesus as our substitutional sacrifice and the payment for all our sins.

"IN AND THROUGH HIM"

> *For our sake He made Christ [virtually] to be sin Who knew no sin, so that **in and through Him** we might become [endued with, viewed as being in, and examples of] the righteousness of God [what we ought to be, approved and acceptable and in right relationship with Him, by His goodness].*
> *2 Corinthians 5:21*

God chooses to see us as "right" because He wants to see us that way. Ephesians 1:4,5 teaches us that God chose to love us and to view us as blameless because He wanted to do so, because it pleased Him:

> *Even as [in His love] He chose us [actually picked us out for Himself as His own] **in Christ** before the foundation of the world, that we should be holy (consecrated and set apart for Him) and blameless in His sight, even above reproach, before Him in love.*
> *For He foreordained us (destined us, planned in love for us) to be adopted (revealed) as His own children **through Jesus Christ,** in accordance with the purpose of His will [because it pleased Him and was His kind intent].*

When I teach on this subject, I always think of the relationship between my husband and my son. My oldest son David is the child of a previous marriage. I was married at age eighteen. In my childhood I had been sexually abused, and the nineteen-year-old I married had not been properly corrected. He was a smooth-talking, take-advantage-of-everyone type of guy. I was insecure and desperate for real love. He told me he loved me, and since I was afraid nobody would ever want me, I grabbed the opportunity to get married even though I knew deep down inside the marriage would not work. My young husband was unfaithful, and most of the time he did not work. After five years of rejection and other emotional pain, I divorced him. From that marriage we had one child, a son whom I named after my only brother, David. When the boy was nine months old, I met Dave Meyer, who was to become my husband of more than thirty years.

David was adopted by Dave. Dave chose to love and accept David before David accepted him, before he even had a relationship with him, or really even knew him. Dave and I had a fast courtship. After about five dates, he asked me to marry him. He was a born-again, Spirit-filled Christian who was praying for a wife. He asked God to give him someone who needed help! He certainly got his prayers answered when he got me. He was being led by the Spirit of God in our relationship. He says that he knew the first night he saw me that I was going to be his wife. He likes a challenge and could tell right away that I would be one.

The night Dave asked me to marry him, I asked him about my son. I did not know how he felt about David. Dave's answer was precious and depicts the way God feels about us. He said, "Even though I don't know David very well, I love him because I love you and anything that is part of you."

This is the same way we enter into a loving relationship with God wherein He accepts us because of His own goodness and not ours. He has accepted Christ and His substitutionary work on the cross, and He accepts us because, as believers, we are "in Christ."

The following is a partial list of the things that are now ours by virtue of being "in Christ":

> ...blessing...be to the God and Father of our Lord Jesus Christ (the Messiah) Who has blessed us **in Christ** with every spiritual...blessing in the heavenly realm!
> Ephesians 1:3

> [So that we might be] to the praise and the commendation of His glorious grace (favor and mercy), which He so freely bestowed on us **in the Beloved.**
> Ephesians 1:6

> **In Him** we have redemption (deliverance and salvation) through His blood, the remission (forgiveness) of our offenses (shortcomings and trespasses), in accordance with the riches and the generosity of His gracious favor.
> Ephesians 1:7

> **In Him** we also were made [God's] heritage (portion) and we obtained an inheritance....
> Ephesians 1:11

> **In Him** you also who have heard the Word of Truth, the glad tidings (Gospel) of your salvation, and have believed in and adhered to and relied on Him, were stamped with the seal of the long-promised Holy Spirit.
> Ephesians 1:13

> Even when we were dead (slain) by [our own] shortcomings and trespasses, He made us alive together **in fellowship and in union with Christ;** [He gave us the very life of Christ Himself, the same new life with which He quickened Him, for] it is by grace (His favor and mercy which you did not

deserve) that you are saved (delivered from judgment and made partakers of Christ's salvation).
Ephesians 2:5

*For it is **through Him** that we both [whether far off or near] now have an introduction (access) by one [Holy] Spirit to the Father [so that we are able to approach Him].*
Ephesians 2:18

***In Him**...you yourselves also are being built up....*
Ephesians 2:22

*Have the roots [of your being] firmly and deeply planted **[in Him**, fixed and founded **in Him]**, being continually built up **in Him**, becoming increasingly more confirmed and established in the faith, just as you were taught, and abounding and overflowing in it with thanksgiving.*
Colossians 2:7

*And you are **in Him**, made full and having come to fullness of life **[in Christ** you too are filled with the Godhead — Father, Son and Holy Spirit —...].*
Colossians 2:10

This is a very small portion of the many Scriptures that make this reference, but I trust that you can see from these examples how important it is to have a full understanding of the difference between being "in Christ" and doing works to earn favor.

Actually it is impossible to "earn favor"; otherwise, it would not be favor. A favor is something someone does for us out of kindness, not because we deserve it.

RESTORING OUR WORTH AND VALUE

Look out for those dogs [Judaizers, legalists], look out for those mischief-makers, look out for those who mutilate the flesh.

For we [Christians] are the true circumcision, who worship
God in spirit and by the Spirit of God and exult and glory
and pride ourselves in Jesus Christ, and put no confidence or
dependence [on what we are] in the flesh and on outward
privileges and physical advantages and external appearances.
Philippians 3:2,3

This passage destroys any reason to believe that our confidence can be in anything we can do or have done. It clearly tells us that our confidence cannot be "in the flesh," but instead must be "in Christ Jesus." It also warns us to beware of legalists.

It is freeing to finally see that our worth and value are not based on what we do, but on who we are in Christ. God has assigned value to us by allowing Jesus to die for us. By the very act of Christ's death on the cross, and the suffering He endured, God the Father is saying to each one of us, "You are very valuable to Me, and I will pay any price to redeem you and see that you have the good life I originally intended for you."

Once you and I have our "who" straightened out, then and only then can we begin to effectively pray about our "do."

You might say, "But, Joyce, I can't believe that God doesn't care about what we do!"

You are right. God does care about our actions. He wants them to be correct. He actually wants us to grow up and become mature Christians who act like Jesus did when He walked the earth. God wants us to do good works — but He does not want us to depend on them to gain us anything. He wants us to do good works because we love Him. He wants our good works to be a response to what He has done to, for and in us.

Once I knew who I was in Christ, then I began doing good works for *right reasons.*

Many people do good works for wrong reasons, and get no reward for them.

Our motives are of utmost importance to God. I can remember even reading my Bible daily, thinking in my heart that God would be pleased or impressed if I read huge amounts of it each day. Because I was reading for the wrong reason, my reading was a bondage to me rather than a joy. Reading the Bible daily and making sure I read a certain amount became a law to me. If I did not do it, I felt guilty.

The Lord revealed to me one day that I was reading with wrong motives. He placed this thought in my heart: "God knows the Bible. I am not reading it for Him; I am doing it for me so I can know what He wants me to do and go do it."

The Lord showed me that to read one verse of Scripture, and truly have understanding about it, is better than reading ten chapters and not remembering anything we have read. In our society today we are too impressed with quantity and not concerned enough about quality!

I was so engrossed in what I was supposed to "do," that I forgot to simply "be." We are called *human beings* because we are supposed to be; otherwise, we would be called *human doings*.

Satan regularly screams in our ears, "What are you going to *do?*" "You have to *do* something!" "You had better *do* something!" Actually, he is right, there is something we should do — *believe!* We should always be believing.

YOUR "WHO" WILL FIX YOUR "DO" ─────────────

Let me ask you this one question: Did you receive the [Holy] Spirit as the result of obeying the Law and doing its works, or was it by hearing [the message of the Gospel] and believing [it]? [Was it from observing a law of rituals or from a message of faith?]

*Are you so foolish and so senseless and so silly? Having
begun [your new life spiritually] with the [Holy] Spirit, are
you now reaching perfection [by dependence] on the flesh?
Have you suffered so many things and experienced so much
all for nothing (to no purpose) — if it really is to no purpose
and in vain?*
Galatians 3:2-4

I was doing a lot of things wrong, and I had many wrong attitudes. I desperately needed to change, and I wanted to. *I was trying!* But nothing was working. I felt condemned all the time. I felt like a failure as a Christian. I was sure that everyone else was so much better than I was, how could God ever use me?

I was concentrating on the wrong thing!

I kept looking at what was wrong with me when I should have been developing a relationship with the Lord. I suppose I thought that He really did not want much to do with me until I was all "fixed up." I knew He had saved me, but fellowship was another thing entirely. When I did find time to be with God, I spent most of it telling Him how terrible I was and how sorry I was for being so terrible. Then I would promise to do better, but I never could find the way.

Finally I saw it! In Romans 8:1, I received a revelation regarding the righteousness that comes through Christ Jesus: *Therefore, [there is] now no condemnation (no adjudging guilty of wrong) for those who are in Christ Jesus...* [that sounded so good to me, but then I saw the rest of it]... *who live [and] walk not after the dictates of the flesh, but after the dictates of the Spirit.* Now I was back to square one. Certainly, if I could walk after the Spirit all the time, there would be no condemnation, but I was not able to do that; so where did it leave me?

Then God revealed this to me for my life: Yes, if I walk after the Spirit instead of the flesh, there will be no condemnation. But when I do sin (which we all do), there is a "fleshly way" of handling it and a "spiritual way." I was handling mine the fleshly way. I would get fleshly and sin (perhaps lose my temper, or say things I should not have said), but then I would stay in the flesh trying to be forgiven. I was *doing* things to make up for what I had done wrong instead of accepting forgiveness as a free gift. Once I received that gift, I was free to do good things because I was overwhelmed by God's love and mercy for me, because my heart was so full of love for Him that it overflowed in good works.

My problem was that I wanted to change, but I had my "who" and my "do" mixed up. I was trying to "do" so my "who" would be right. But I actually needed to know "who" I was in Christ, and then He would help me "do" right things for right reasons.

This is not a modern-day problem. Paul addressed the issue frequently. In his letter to the Galatians he asked them why they were trying to reach perfection by dependence upon the flesh. He urged them to remember that their entire new spiritual life was given birth because of faith and leaning on the Holy Spirit; therefore, why would they need to try to reach perfection any way other than how they began?

He concluded by telling them that if they did not stop this type of legalistic behavior, everything they had suffered so far would be to no purpose and in vain.

I don't know about you, but I have come too far and gone through too much to mess it all up now. I want to know the right way to approach God, and as far as I can see in His Word, it is through faith in what Jesus has done, not faith in what I can do.

We cannot succeed at being ourselves without knowing these things. We cannot succeed without stepping out *in faith, not works*. If we believe our acceptance is based on our doing, we will always feel rejected when we fail to do the right thing. But if we put our dependence on who we are in Christ, rather than on what we do for Him, our "who" will fix our "do."

FROM GLORY TO GLORY

> *But we all, with unveiled face, beholding as in a mirror the glory of the Lord, are being transformed into the same image **from glory to glory**, just as by the Spirit of the Lord.*
> 2 Corinthians 3:18 NKJV

Let's go back to the original question posed in the introduction to this book:

How do you see yourself?

Are you able to honestly evaluate yourself and your behavior and not come under condemnation? Are you able to look at how far you still have to go, but also look at how far you have come? Where you are now is not where you will end up. Have a vision for the finish line or you will never get out of the starting block.

In *The Amplified Bible* version of 2 Corinthians 3:18, Paul states that God changes us *from one degree of glory to another.* In other words, the changes in us personally, as well as those in our circumstances, take place in degrees.

You are in a glory right now!

If you are born again, then you are somewhere on the path of the righteous. You may not be as far along as you would like to be, but thank God you are on the path. There was a time when you were totally outside of covenant relationship with God through unbelief. (Ephesians 2:11,12.) But now you belong to the household of God and are being transformed by Him day by day. Enjoy the glory you are in right now and don't get jealous of where others may be. They had to pass through where you are at some time themselves.

We have a strong (fleshly) tendency to compare our glory with everybody else's. The devil arranges for us to think that way, but it is not God's way. God wants us to realize that each of us is a unique individual and that He has a unique plan for every one of us. Satan wants to make sure that we never enjoy where we are at the moment. He wants us in competition with one another, always wanting what someone else has. When we don't know how to enjoy the glory we are in right now, all we do is slow down the maturity process. I don't believe we pass into the next degree of glory until we have learned to enjoy the one we are in at the moment.

In this sense, a "glory" is simply a place that is better than the previous one.

I had so many flaws in my personality and character that even after five years of trying to walk with the Lord, I still felt that I had made practically no progress. Yet, all that time I was gradually becoming a little more glorious.

We are usually too hard on ourselves. We would grow faster if we relaxed more. We cannot live by our feelings in these matters. Satan makes sure we frequently "feel" that we are an unredeemable mess or that God is not working in our lives. We must learn to live by God's Word and not by how we feel. His Word states that as long we believe, He is working in us!

WE ARE A "WORK IN PROGRESS"————————————

> ...the Word of God...is effectually at work in you who believe
> [exercising its superhuman power in those who adhere to and
> trust in and rely on it].
> 1 Thessalonians 2:13

I encourage you to say every day, "God is working in me right now — He is changing me!" Speak out of your mouth what the Word says, not what you feel.

It seems that we incessantly talk about how we feel. When we do that, it is difficult for the Word of God to work in us effectively. We magnify our feelings about everything else and allow them to take the lead role in our lives.

Often we "feel" rejected, so we believe people are rejecting us. Perhaps the truth is they do not even see us; therefore, they are not accepting or rejecting us. If we believe that people are rejecting us, it is likely that they will reject us. Our "poor me, nobody loves me, I'm always rejected" attitude is what makes people want to stay away from us.

We must not develop the attitude that if we don't perform perfectly, we will be rejected. I will admit that the world often operates on that principle, but God doesn't, and neither should we. None of us who has taken an honest look at ourselves would dare refuse to accept others unless they are perfect. Jesus taught that we can demand perfection in others as a prerequisite to relationship with us only when our own perfection is complete.

We become so accustomed to people in the world being overly concerned about our performance and what we are doing, that we bring wrong thinking into our relationship with God through Jesus Christ. We think God is the way the world is, and He is not. The fear of being rejected (or not being accepted) is one of the major hindrances to our succeeding at being ourselves.

As we step out to be all we can be in Christ, we will make some mistakes — everyone does. But it takes the pressure off of us when we realize that God is expecting us to do the best we can. He is not expecting us to be perfect (totally without flaw). If we were as perfect as we try to be, we would not need a Savior. I believe God will always leave a certain number of defects in us, just so we will know how much we need Jesus every single day.

I am not a perfect preacher. There are times when I say things wrong, times when I believe I have heard from God and find out I was hearing from myself. There are many times when I fall short of perfection (like several hundred times every day!). I don't have perfect faith, a perfect attitude, perfect thoughts and perfect ways.

Jesus knew that would happen to all of us. That is why He "stands in the gap" for us. (Ezekiel 22:30.) A gap is a space between two things. There is a gap, a space between us and God put there by our imperfections and sins. God is perfect and completely holy. He can only fellowship with those who are like Him. That is why we come to Him through Christ. Jesus is just like His Father. He has told us, "If you have seen Me, you have seen the Father." (John 14:9, author's paraphrase.)

Jesus stands in the gap between God's perfection and our imperfection. He *continually* intercedes for us because we *continually* need it. (Hebrews 7:25.) Jesus came to us as both the Son of God and the Son of Man. He is the Mediator between the two parties — us and God. (1 Timothy 2:5.) Through Him, we come into agreement and fellowship with the Father. In Him we are acceptable to God.

ACCEPTED IN THE BELOVED

> *...he hath made us accepted in the beloved.*
> *Ephesians 1:6 KJV*

We do not have to believe that God accepts us only if we perform perfectly. We can believe the truth that He accepts us "in the Beloved."

God accepts us because we are believers in His Son Jesus Christ. If we believe the lies of Satan, we spend our lives struggling and in frustration. Our abilities are crippled, and we never succeed at being ourselves.

God spoke to my heart once and said, "Do your best, then enter My rest." That sounded very good to me, because I had tried everything else and was completely worn out. I have found that my best each day still includes some imperfections, but that is why Jesus died for you and me.

THE PERFORMANCE/ACCEPTANCE TREADMILL —————

> *But to one who, not working [by the Law], trusts (believes fully) in Him Who justifies the ungodly, his faith is credited to him as righteousness (the standing acceptable to God). Thus David congratulates the man and pronounces a blessing on him to whom God credits righteousness apart from the works he does.*
> *Romans 4:5,6*

If we spend years on the performance/acceptance treadmill, it is hard to get off of it. It becomes a way of living. It affects our thoughts, perceptions and decisions.

Many people would rather stay on the performance/acceptance treadmill than step off it and have to face the possibility of failure. Others feel so bad about themselves due to their past failures that they won't even try to start a new way of life.

When people are addicted to feeling good about themselves only when they perform well, they are in for a life of misery. It is a cycle of trying and failing, trying harder and failing again, feeling guilty and rejected, trying again and failing again, and on and on.

God does not want us on the performance/acceptance treadmill. He wants us to feel good about ourselves whether we perform perfectly or not. He doesn't want us to be filled with pride, but He certainly did not create us to reject ourselves. This is where a revelation concerning our "who" and our "do" is so valuable. We should be able to separate the two and take an honest look at both. If we perform poorly, we can be sorry and hope to do better the next time. We can try to improve our performance (our "do"), but our worth and value (our "who") cannot be determined by our performance.

People who have problems in this area perceive things wrongly. If they are expecting to be rejected when their performance is not good, they react as though they were already rejected — which confuses those in relationship with them.

Here is an example. My general manager, who has been with us many years, had a problem in the area of performance/acceptance. She grew up believing and receiving the message that she gained acceptance and love through perfection.

When she first began working for us, we noticed that anytime we asked her about her workload she would react very strangely. It seemed to upset her and throw her into a cycle of working harder and more furiously, unless she was able to tell us that everything was perfectly caught up and all her workload was completed. This behavior was becoming a big problem for me because I felt her withdraw and actually reject me during those times. I was not rejecting her because of her imperfection, but she believed she was being rejected by me; therefore, she could not *receive* my love, which I still wanted to freely give her.

We receive through the act of believing; what we believe is what we receive, and nothing else. If we don't believe in the grace, mercy and favor of God, then we cannot receive it. If we believe we must do everything perfectly right to be accepted by God, then we will reject His love even though He is not rejecting us. This wrong thinking and believing keeps us trapped. It is like a treadmill that is going so fast we cannot seem to find a place to get off.

If you are trapped on the performance/acceptance treadmill, I pray that the cycle will be broken in your life so you can freely receive God's acceptance and then help others do the same.

TAKE THE PRESSURE OFF OTHER PEOPLE

> *They tie up heavy loads, hard to bear, and place them on men's shoulders, but they themselves will not lift a finger to help bear them.*
> *Matthew 23:4*

You and I pressure ourselves when we have unrealistic expectations, when we expect ourselves to be perfect. God does not want us to live under this kind of pressure.

We also can fall into wrong thinking that causes us to pressure other people. We can expect more out of people than they are able to give us. Continued pressure on people we are in relationship with will ultimately cause the collapse of that relationship.

All people everywhere are looking for acceptance.

As humans, all of us require space, or freedom, to be who we are. We want to be accepted as we are. That does not mean that we don't know we need some change, but we don't want people giving us the message, even subtly, that we must change in order to be "in."

We are more likely to change for those who are willing to accept us with our flaws, than we are for those who make demands and expect us to live by their list of rules and regulations.

One thing is for sure, God won't change the people we are trying to change. He has a "hands off policy" when He is working in human lives.

I remember the years I furiously tried to change my husband Dave and each of our children in different ways. Those were frustrating years, because no matter what I tried, it didn't work! One day God told me, "Either you're going to do this, or I am, but we are not both going to do it. I'll wait until you're finished. When you are, let Me know, and I will go to work and get the job done!"

My family knew I was not satisfied with them. I loved them, but not unconditionally. I wasn't willing to accept their flaws: *I was going to change them!*

Even when we think we are hiding our disapproval, people can still feel it. It is in our voice tone and body language even when it isn't in our words. We may try to control what we say, but whatever is in the heart eventually comes out of the mouth. Sooner or later we slip and say what we have been thinking.

I was pressuring my family, and the fact that I would not accept them the way they were was pressuring me.

I am not saying that we must accept sin and wrong behavior in other people and merely put up with it. But I am saying loud and clear, from my own personal experience and from God's Word, that *the way to change is prayer, not pressure!* If we love people and pray about their sin, God will work.

Many people who irritate us are simply being themselves, and their personality just does not mesh with ours.

My oldest son David, for example, made me feel continually that I had to prove to him that I loved him. He challenged me about almost everything. It wasn't that he refused to do what he was told to do, but he had to challenge it. He wanted control, and I wasn't willing to give it up. He was opinionated, and I didn't like it. He was quick tempered and impatient, and I did not like that either. He could walk in the room where I was, and within a few minutes we would be in some type of conflict. Even if it wasn't verbal, we could still feel the strife in the atmosphere.

I loved my son, but I didn't like him. I wanted him to change, and I was determined that he was going to do so whether he wanted to or not. Needless to say, our relationship was under constant pressure. As he got older, our conflict worsened, but since he was a man and no longer a boy, I had no recourse but to accept him as he was or else ask him to move out of the house.

One night in a mid-week church service, the Lord revealed to me that I was holding unforgiveness against my son because I didn't think he was spiritual enough. I wanted him (and all my children) to be "very spiritual." I also wanted him to "act the part" in church and around my friends. I wanted him to spend his evenings reading the Bible. I wanted to hear him praying in the morning. I wanted, I wanted, I wanted — and all I got was frustration and pressure.

God told me to apologize to David for the years of pressure I had placed upon him and for not accepting him as he was. It took me a couple of weeks to obey. I was afraid that if I humbled myself and did as God was asking, my son would take advantage of the situation.

Finally, I did as God commanded me. I told my son what God had shown me and apologized to him. With my husband Dave, we told David that he was eighteen years old, and we needed to lay down some new household guidelines, so we took this opportunity to do so. We told him that we wanted him to go to church once a week, not to bring girls to the house when we were not there, and not to play hard rock music in the house when we were gone. Other than that, we were willing to back off and stop trying to change him. We told him we accepted him the way he was.

When Dave and I explained all this to our son, he began to cry.

"You don't know how bad I've needed to hear that you love me and accept me the way I am," he said. Then he went on to say, "I wish with all my heart that I felt about God the way you and Dad do, but I don't, and I can't make myself feel any different. I am doing the best I can right now, but I hope to change."

It took a lot of grace, especially on my part, but we did take the pressure off. We backed off and put our trust in God to do what needed to be done. About six months went by, and we saw no change in David. Then *suddenly* one New Year's Eve he went to church, and God touched him! When he came home he announced that he was going to Bible college and that he was going to serve God fully, even if it meant that he would lose every friend he had.

Now David is one of our division managers at Life In The Word. He is the head of our World Missions program and the media department. He is also one of our good friends. We enjoy our fellowship together.

While I was pressuring David, it had a boomerang effect and actually ended up pressuring me. It did no good, but actually did harm — to our relationship and to his level of security. It was many years after the fact that I finally realized why I had such a hard time with his personality: *he is just like me!*

My husband's personality irritated me also. Dave is easygoing (about most things). He is a peace lover and will go the extra mile to preserve it. His philosophy of life is taken straight from the Bible — *cast your care!* (1 Peter 5:7.) That is his answer to most things. As a result, life is fairly easy for him.

I, on the other hand, was not easygoing about anything. I had very definite opinions and desires. When I didn't get my way, I made a lot of noise about it. I did care and was not willing to cast it.

Dave's easygoing nature, although a great blessing to me, also aggravated me at times. I thought I wanted him to be more aggressive in life. One day he set me straight when he said to me, "Joyce, you had better be very happy that I am the way I am; otherwise, you sure wouldn't be doing what you're doing." He was talking about my being in full-time ministry. The fact that God has made Dave the way he is has made it easy for him to allow me the freedom to succeed at being myself. He has not only allowed me — he has helped me.

Often the things we need the most in other people are available for us to enjoy, *if* we will stop judging them and trying to change them. I needed a peaceful man in my life. All the other men I had encountered had been anything but peaceful. I had prayed for years for a man like Dave, and when I got him I tried to put him on the potter's wheel and remold him. It caused pressure in our relationship.

Dave was easygoing, but even he finally got tired of it. He was beginning not to like me anymore — he told me so, and it frightened me. I
am glad it did, because it provoked me to take the pressure off and
trust God to change what needed changing.

Dave has always loved sports, and that was one of the things I
wanted to change. I did not care for them, so in my selfishness I
wanted him not to like them either. I wanted all of his attention. I
wanted him to do what I wanted to do.

I, I, I — that is our biggest problem.

I remember many Sunday afternoons that were spent with me
angry and pouting while Dave watched football, baseball, hockey, golf
or some other sport. My attitude did not stop him from watching
them; as a matter of fact, he really did not allow me to bother him at
all, and that made me even madder. But eventually it ministered to me.
I became very hungry for the stability and peace that I saw in his life.

As the years went by, I learned that I could find other things to
do during those ball games. Dave did things that I wanted him to do
most of the time. It was unrealistic for me to expect him to give up
everything he enjoyed just because I didn't enjoy it.

I have come a long way. Right now as I write this book, I am
looking at Dave who is sitting across the room from where I am
working on my computer. He is watching a golf match and at
commercials he is watching a football game. He has not changed in
that area, but I have. The pressure is gone, and our marriage is better.

Sometimes we want others to change, when actually we are the
ones who need to change.

Our oldest daughter, Laura, was undisciplined. She did not like
school and was satisfied with mediocre to poor grades. Her room was
always a mess, and I was constantly telling her (actually screaming at

her) to clean it up. I did not like her choice of friends, nor did I like her attitude. I pressured her so much that by the time she got married, she didn't call me for six months. That hurt me very badly, but I understand now some things I did not understand then.

We cannot change people by pressuring them or by nagging them.

For change to be lasting, it must come from the inside out. Only God can effect that type of heart change.

Thank God, Laura and I have a restored relationship also. After six months she told me that I had been right about a lot of things. By that time I was willing to admit that I had also been wrong about a lot of things. Today she works on our staff, as do all of our children, and she and I are very good friends.

She has changed, and I have changed, but we didn't change each other. God did it all!

My youngest daughter, Sandra, was not as hard for me to handle as the two older children. Her personality made her want to do everything perfectly, and the more perfect she was, the better I liked it. She pressured herself enough that she needed no help from anyone else. She had a lot of unrealistic expectations of herself that pressured her to the point of having stress-related back problems and colon problems. She was never satisfied with herself in anything. She didn't like her hair, her skin, her looks or her figure. She didn't like her gifts and talents. She thought she was slow and dumb. She has also changed! It seems that we all change if we "hang in there" with the Lord.

Sandra is now in charge of the helps ministry for our conferences. It is a big responsibility, and she does an outstanding job. She also helps me with some things in the pulpit (offerings, announcements, exhortations, and so forth). She has a genuine call on her life to the helps ministry. She absolutely loves to help! She helps her brothers and sisters by baby-sitting for them. She helps my widowed aunt by spending time with her and taking her places.

The devil had Sandra convinced in the early years of her life that she was not gifted or talented. She believed him, and as long as she did so, she was miserable and felt worthless. What a liar Satan is, but as long as we believe his lies, we are unfulfilled and never succeed at being ourselves.

Sandra was and is, a precious individual who rejected herself for a period of time, but through God's Word found truth that has made her free. Her perfectionist personality caused her to pressure other people for a while. She had unrealistic expectations of them just as she did of herself.

Anytime we expect someone else to keep us happy all the time, we are in for some disappointment.

When Sandra got married, it was to a man who is a lot like Dave — very easygoing and a lover of peace. He is very easy to get along with, but he does not like to be nagged. He came to a point where he told Sandra to stop acting like his mother. She was very mad and hurt, but as the days went by she realized he was right. She has taken the pressure off of him, and as a result is experiencing less pressure herself.

Our youngest son Daniel missed most of my "fiery days." By the time he came along, I was more mature in the Lord. I had learned the lessons of accepting people as they are, allowing God to make the changes in them He deems necessary.

Daniel's personality is a lot like Laura's, but he and I have had very little conflict in all these years. I accept him because of who he is, not because of what he does or does not do. I correct him when he needs it, but I don't reject him because he has not pleased me.

Like Laura, Daniel did not like school, and all twelve years it was push and shove to get him through — but he made it. He graduated and is a regular member of society now. He works in the television department of our ministry and has a vision to work with youth. I am so glad that I finally learned how to be peaceful.

Peace is much better than pressure!

Perhaps you need to take the pressure off of some people in your life. Think it over. If God shows you situations where you are out of balance in this area, I urge you to make the necessary changes.

You and I reap what we sow, as does everyone else. If we sow freedom in other people's lives, we will reap freedom. If we take the pressure off of others, we will not only take the pressure off of ourselves, but we will notice other people pressuring us less also.

UNREALISTIC EXPECTATIONS

> *And He did not need anyone to bear witness concerning man [needed no evidence from anyone about men], for He Himself knew what was in human nature. [He could read men's hearts.]*
> *John 2:25*

We have discussed unrealistic expectations concerning people to some extent, but I want to take a deeper look at the subject. It seems that our expectations are what sets us up for disappointment with people and situations.

Am I saying, then, that we should not expect anything? Of course not! We should expect the best out of people, but at the same time we must remember they are people.

When Jesus' disciples disappointed Him, it did not devastate Him because He already knew and fully understood human nature. Jesus expected His disciples to do their best, but He knew that even their best would still be imperfect.

I have come to realize that we are always looking for the perfect marriage, perfect friend, perfect job, perfect neighborhood, perfect church, and the truth is, *it does not exist!* As long as we are in earthly bodies we will manifest imperfection. God must have known that to be true, because He gave us many instructions in His Word regarding how to handle people who irritate us or disappoint us.

For example, in Galatians 6:2, we read: *Bear (endure, carry) one another's burdens and troublesome moral faults, and in this way fulfill and observe perfectly the law of Christ (the Messiah) and complete what is lacking [in your obedience to it].*

In John 13:34 Jesus said, *I give you a new commandment: that you should love one another. Just as I have loved you, so you too should love one another.* The law of Christ is the law of love. If we love one another as He loves us, then we must love without conditions and without pressure.

In 1 Peter 2:19-21, Peter tells us that we are to love those who are difficult to get along with, saying further that we are actually called to this type of life.

Another Scripture that teaches us how to treat those who hurt or irritate us is Romans 12:16, in which Paul writes: *Live in harmony with one another; do not be haughty (snobbish, high-minded, exclusive), but readily adjust yourself to [people, things] and give yourselves to humble tasks. Never overestimate yourself or be wise in your own conceits.*

Finally, 1 Peter 3:9 tells us, *Never return evil for evil or insult for insult (scolding, tongue-lashing, berating), but on the contrary blessing [praying for their welfare, happiness, and protection, and truly pitying and loving them]. For know that to this you have been called, that you may yourselves inherit a blessing [from God — that you may obtain a blessing as heirs, bringing welfare and happiness and protection].*

There is no place in God's Word that we are told to reject people. Instead, we are to love them, we are to give them understanding, mercy and compassion.

I admit it is easier to talk about how to treat the irritating people in our lives than it is to do it, but if the Lord has told us to do it, then we can do it.

Unrealistic expectations affect us in many different areas. First, we have unrealistic expectations of ourselves. We expect that we should be able to do what others do. Yet if we are not gifted in some area, we cannot excel in it. When we do things poorly, we feel bad about ourselves. That seems to set in motion a never-ending cycle of reaching for things that are out of our reach, hoping to prove something that we don't have to prove at all.

I am free to be me, and you are free to be you. All we need to do is personally obey God, we don't need to prove anything to ourselves or anyone else. If we obey God, He will take care of our reputation. When we expect to perform in areas outside of our gifting and calling, we set ourselves up for major disappointment.

Unrealistic expectations also affect us in our relationships with other people. As we have already mentioned, people are people, and all people come with strengths and weaknesses. To be in relationship with people we have to take both. To expect others to be responsible for our personal happiness is a big mistake.

As Abraham Lincoln said, most people are about as happy as they make up their mind to be. If they don't decide to be happy, we can't keep them happy, no matter what we do.

During the years that I had all the unrealistic expectations of Dave and my children, I frustrated everyone with my unreasonable demands. Dave, being a peace lover, tried to keep me happy by doing the various things I said I wanted done, but somehow I was never permanently happy. Finally, one day he said, "Joyce, I have realized that no matter what I do, I cannot keep you happy; therefore, I am through trying."

I was not happy because I was not looking at life realistically.

There are times when we like to believe that faith removes realism, that no matter what is going on in our lives, we can reverse it by believing God to change it. Many things can be changed by God's power and His Word, but there are some issues in life we must face and deal with ourselves, and one of those issues is what I am talking about right now.

People are not perfect, and to expect them to be is frustrating for everyone involved. We must learn to be generous with mercy and to sow seeds of mercy so we can reap mercy when we need it.

Unrealistic expectations concerning our circumstances can also be a tool used by Satan to bring us into discouragement and despair. In John 16:33 NKJV Jesus said, "...*In the world you will have tribulation; but be of good cheer, I have overcome the world.*" What was He saying? "You might as well cheer up because as long as you are in the world you will have some tribulation. But don't worry about it, because I have everything under control."

We all like to plan our life and have it go exactly the way we planned, but that rarely happens. That is not negative — it is truth. As believers, we are given the power of the Holy Spirit to help us do difficult things, not to make our life so easy that we never have to use our faith.

I urge you to expect good things to happen in your life. I certainly would not tell you to expect bad things. I also urge you to be realistic and realize that we all have to deal with things that are unpleasant and people who are disagreeable. Our attitude in these trying situations makes the difference between whether we enjoy life or not.

I encourage you to set your mind and keep it set in this area. Be determined never to be defeated again by circumstances that don't line up with your desires. Stay calm in trials and trust God. What Satan intends for your harm, God will work for your good as you trust Him. Pray in this area and ask for the help of the Holy Spirit. As long as you live in the deception of unrealistic expectations, you will never succeed at being yourself.

8

RECEIVING GRACE, FAVOR AND MERCY

8
RECEIVING GRACE, FAVOR AND MERCY

There are some words in the Bible that I like to call "power words." If these words are understood correctly, they can greatly help us succeed at being ourselves. Just as we can never be free to succeed at being ourselves unless we learn about and receive God's unconditional love, so it is with receiving His grace, favor and mercy.

> **Let us then fearlessly and confidently and boldly draw near to the throne of *grace* (the throne of God's unmerited *favor* to us sinners), that we may *receive mercy* [for our failures] and find *grace* to help in good time for every need [appropriate help and well-timed help, coming just when we need it].**
> **HEBREWS 4:16**

First, let's examine the power word *receive*.

I mentioned that we must receive grace, favor and mercy, but many people don't know how to receive at all. We are accustomed in our society to working or paying for everything. We struggle to get, but God wants us to freely receive.

Even in our conversations with one another we say things like: "Did you *get* saved? Did you *get* the Holy Spirit? Did you *get* a breakthrough? Did you *get* free?" These are really inappropriate questions, but are indicative of our mindsets.

Again and again, the Bible speaks of receiving from God. He is always pouring out His blessing, and we should, as empty, thirsty vessels, learn to take in freely all that He offers us. Consider these Scriptures:

> *But to as many as did **receive** and welcome Him, He gave the authority (power, privilege, right) to become the children of God, that is, to those who believe in (adhere to, trust in, and rely on) His name.*
> *John 1:12*

*For out of His fullness (abundance) we have all **received** [all had a share and we were all supplied with] one grace after another and spiritual blessing upon spiritual blessing and even favor upon favor and gift [heaped] upon gift.*
John 1:16

*But you shall **receive** power (ability, efficiency, and might) when the Holy Spirit has come upon you, and you shall be My witnesses in Jerusalem and all Judea and Samaria and to the ends (the very bounds) of the earth.*
Acts 1:8

*Then [the apostles] laid their hands on them one by one, and they **received** the Holy Spirit.*
Acts 8:17

*To Him all the prophets testify (bear witness) that everyone who believes in Him [who adheres to, trusts in, and relies on Him, giving himself up to Him] **receives** forgiveness of sins through His name.*
Acts 10:43

*...we beg of you not to **receive** the grace of God in vain....*
2 Corinthians 6:1

*Let me ask you this one question: Did you **receive** the [Holy] Spirit as the result of obeying the Law and doing its works, or was it by hearing [the message of the Gospel] and believing [it]?...*
Galatians 3:2

*As you have therefore **received** Christ, [even] Jesus the Lord, [so] walk (regulate your lives and conduct yourselves) in union with and conformity to Him.*
Colossians 2:6

*...that we may **receive** mercy [for our failures]....*
Hebrews 4:16

*So get rid of all uncleanness and the rampant outgrowth of wickedness, and in a humble (gentle, modest) spirit **receive** and welcome the Word which implanted and rooted [in your hearts] contains the power to save your souls.*
James 1:21

These Scriptures and many others like them bring out the principle of receiving rather than getting. My studies over the years have produced these definitions of the words *get* and *receive:* To get is to obtain by struggle and effort, while to receive is to become a receptacle and simply take in what is being offered.

This distinction between getting and receiving helps us understand why so many Christians struggle in their walk with the Lord. They are trying to get everything they need from Him when they should be simply asking and receiving.

ASKING AND RECEIVING

"...Ask, and you will receive, that your joy may be full."
John 16:24 NKJV

This is one of my favorite Scriptures on the subject of receiving. It sounds so simple, and actually it is meant to be so.

Jesus came to deliver us from struggling, not to invite us to a new way of struggling under the banner of Christianity. When we learn to ask and receive, truly our joy will be full. Once we have freely received, then we can freely give.

FREELY RECEIVE, FREELY GIVE

"...Freely you have received, freely give."
Matthew 10:8 NKJV

In our society today we find very few people who are able to freely give. Perhaps this Scripture sheds light on why. If we never learn to freely receive from Jesus, we will never learn to freely give to others.

Satan has done a good job of deceiving us into believing that we must earn or pay for everything. We have somehow been convinced that we must struggle and strive to get what we want from God. Yet Jesus said, *Come unto me, all ye that labour and are heavy laden, and I will **give** you rest* (Matthew 11:28 KJV).

"Come unto Me" is a comfortable feeling invitation. It is not filled with sounds of struggle and effort.

We must learn more about receiving and come to the realization that according to God's Word all of His blessings come by grace, through faith.

BY GRACE, THROUGH FAITH

> *For it is by free grace (God's unmerited favor) that you are saved (delivered from judgment and made partakers of Christ's salvation) through [your] faith. And this [salvation] is not of yourselves [of your own doing, it came not through your own striving], but it is the gift of God;*
> *Not because of works [not the fulfillment of the Law's demands], lest any man should boast. [It is not the result of what anyone can possibly do, so no one can pride himself in it or take glory to himself.]*
> *Ephesians 2:8,9*

We are saved by grace through faith, and we must learn to live our daily lives the same way. Grace is something that cannot possibly be earned, it can only be received as a free gift.

Grace is the power of God to help us in areas in which we cannot help ourselves. In John 15:5 Jesus tells us, *...apart from Me...you can do*

130

nothing. Therefore, we need help in every area of our lives. If we are to live victoriously, we must realize our impotence and exercise our faith in God's grace. He is more than willing to help us if we are willing to give up our independent attitudes.

In Galatians 2:21 the Apostle Paul said that if he did not receive the grace of God, he would be treating His gift as something of minor importance, defeating its purpose and nullifying its effect. Grace is always flowing to us in every situation, but it must be received by faith. In verse 20 Paul also said that it was no longer he who lived, but Christ Who lived in him, and that the life he was now living, he was living by faith in the Son of God.

I discovered years ago that every time I became frustrated it was because I was trying to do something myself, in my own strength, instead of putting my faith in God and receiving His grace (help). I was frustrated and struggling with something most of time in the early years of my walk with the Lord. Receiving a revelation of God's grace was a major breakthrough for me. I was always "trying" to do something and leaving God out of the loop. I tried to change myself, tried to change my husband and children, tried to get healed, tried to prosper, tried to make my ministry grow and tried to change every circumstance in my life that I did not like. I was frustrated because none of my trying was producing any good results.

God will not permit us to succeed without Him. If He did, we would take the credit that is due Him. If we could change people, we would be changing them to suit our purposes, which would steal their freedom to make their own choices.

I finally learned to pray for what I thought needed to be changed and let God do it His way in His timing. When I began trusting His grace, I entered His rest.

GRACE AND PEACE TO YOU

> *Grace be unto you, and peace, from God our Father, and from*
> *the Lord Jesus Christ.*
> *1 Corinthians 1:3 KJV*

In many of the epistles we find the greeting in the opening verses "grace be unto you, and peace." We cannot enjoy peace unless we understand grace.

Many believers are frustrated in their Christian experience because they don't understand how to freely receive grace, favor, and mercy. They are always working at something, trying to earn what God only gives by grace through faith.

First Peter 5:5 teaches us that He gives grace only to the humble. The humble are those who admit their weakness and total inability to truly succeed without God's help. The proud are always trying to get some credit. They want to think it is their ability that accomplishes what needs to be done. Proud people have difficulty asking, and even more difficulty receiving.

GROW IN GRACE

> *But grow in grace (undeserved favor, spiritual strength) and*
> *recognition and knowledge and understanding of our Lord*
> *and Savior Jesus Christ (the Messiah). To Him [be] glory*
> *(honor, majesty, and splendor) both now and to the day of*
> *eternity. Amen (so be it)!*
> *2 Peter 3:18*

Once we understand grace, we must grow in learning how to receive it in every situation. Trusting God fully is something we grow into. The more we trust God, the stronger we are spiritually. The more we trust ourselves, or even other people and things, the weaker we are spiritually.

I had to practice trusting God for finances. At one point in my ministry, actually at the very beginning, God asked me to trust Him to provide for my family financially without my working outside the home. I knew I needed time to prepare for the ministry He had called me to. Working a full-time job plus being a wife and mother to three small children did not leave me much time to prepare to be an international Bible teacher. As an act of faith and with my husband's consent, I quit my job and began learning to trust God to provide for us. Dave had a good job, but his salary was forty dollars a month less than our bills. This meant we had to have a miracle from God every month just to meet our regular expenses, let alone have anything extra.

I remember what a struggle it was not to go back to work. Each month God did provide, and seeing His faithfulness was exciting, but I was accustomed to taking care of myself — all this "walking by faith" was crucifying my flesh "big time." It was difficult for me to keep practicing trust, but eventually I learned to walk by faith in this area. Gaining that strong foundation in the beginning of our ministry has helped us many times not to panic when we have financial needs in the ministry.

I also had to practice trusting God concerning submission to authority. I had been hurt and mistreated by authority figures in my life, especially male authority figures. Those experiences had left me quite determined to do things my own way and not trust other people. Of course, the Word of God says that wives should submit to their husbands (Ephesians 5:22 KJV; Colossians 3:18 KJV), and I found this to be very difficult. Like most married couples, Dave and I have very different personalities, and I did not agree with many of his opinions and decisions. However, none of this changed God's Word, so I had to learn to submit whether I wanted to or not. Once again, practicing faith in these areas crucified my flesh.

I vividly recall saying to the Lord in a particularly difficult situation for me, "How can You ask me to trust people after the things that have happened to me in my life?"

He replied in my heart, "I am not asking you to trust people, Joyce, I am asking you to trust Me."

He wanted me to trust Him to bring justice in my life in each situation and to realize that if I did not get my own way, then perhaps I was wrong, or perhaps He had a better way or a different timing in mind. Finally, as I practiced over and over in this area, I gained victory.

We only learn to trust God by doing it. We grow in grace by practicing putting our faith in God and receiving His grace in situations that are difficult or impossible for us. Sometimes we put our faith in God, and He gives us grace for a deliverance. At other times we put our faith in God, and He gives us grace to "go through." We must leave that choice to Him and know that either way we can have victory, but only by grace through faith.

If you are struggling with something right now in your life, ask yourself honestly if you are putting your faith in God that His grace will meet the need. Remember, grace is unmerited favor to us sinners. It is God's power coming into our situations to do for us what we cannot do for ourselves.

GRACE GIFTS

For by the grace (unmerited favor of God) given to me I warn everyone among you not to estimate and think of himself more highly than he ought [not to have an exaggerated opinion of his own importance], but to rate his ability with sober judgment, each according to the degree of faith apportioned by God to him.
Romans 12:3

Earlier in the book we discussed the diversity of gifts that God gives to people. These gifts (abilities and talents) come to us by His grace, not by our merit.

In 1 Corinthians 15:10 the Apostle Paul wrote, *But by the grace (the unmerited favor and blessing) of God I am what I am....* If we do not realize that we are what we are by the grace of God, then we will think more highly of ourselves than we should.

Proud people compare themselves to others and feel superior if they are able to do something others cannot do. As Christians, we are to judge ourselves soberly, knowing that without God we cannot do anything of value and that whatever we are able to accomplish is only by His grace. He gives us a measure of His own faith to do whatever He assigns us in life. He gives us abilities by His grace and favor, not by our earning it.

When God revealed to me His call on my life, I was a big mess. I was born again, but very carnal. I had many emotional dysfunctions due to abuse in my past. I had difficulty maintaining healthy relationships, did not walk in the fruit of the Spirit and was very selfish and self-centered, manipulative and controlling, among many other things. There was no visible reason why God should have chosen me to teach His Word and head up an international ministry. He called me by His grace! I still continue to be amazed at His goodness in my life, and I am very thankful.

We cannot be truly thankful or amazed if we don't understand that we are called by God's goodness, not ours.

The grace of God is multifaceted or many-sided as we see in 1 Peter 4:10: *As each of you has received a gift (a particular spiritual talent, a gracious divine endowment), employ it for one another as [befits] good trustees of God's many-sided grace [faithful stewards of the extremely diverse powers and gifts granted to Christians by unmerited favor].*

God's grace manifests in each of us in a different way. For example, I am very disciplined in many areas. I believe I need a gift of discipline to help me fulfill the call of God on my life. I have to discipline myself to work sometimes when others are enjoying entertainment. I have had to discipline myself over the years to study for many thousands of hours in order to teach the Bible accurately. I am very aware that I need to discipline my behavior and emotions at all times because of my love for the Lord and the position He has privileged me to hold.

Moses was not permitted to take the Israelites into the Promised Land due to his unbridled emotion of anger. (Numbers 20:12; Psalm 106:32,33.) In James 3:1,2 the Bible says that teachers are judged by a higher standard and with greater severity than other people:

> *Not many [of you] should become teachers (self-constituted censors and reprovers of others), my brethren, for you know that we [teachers] will be judged by a higher standard and with greater severity [than other people; thus we assume the greater accountability and the more condemnation].*
> *For we all often stumble and fall and offend in many things. And if anyone does not offend in speech [never says the wrong things], he is a fully developed character and a perfect man, able to control his whole body and to curb his entire nature.*

I have a strong conviction that I need to "walk the walk" and not just "talk the talk." As a leader, I must be an example that other people can follow. I have a flesh just like everyone else, and it does not always want to cooperate with me; therefore, I have to discipline myself. It is not always easy, but discipline for me is probably easier than for someone who has a different personality and is called to do something of a different nature.

Grace manifests itself in different ways in different people, but whatever we are good at or successful at is due to the grace of God.

None of us is gifted in every area, and even in those areas in which we are gifted we are rarely perfect.

For example, I believe I am gifted by God with a strong will, but there are times when that strength also becomes my worst enemy. It is good when I need to press through something difficult, but not so good when I want my way, and my strong will keeps pushing for what God is not giving. I find the same thing to be true with my mouth. My mouth is my greatest gift; it is the part of me that God uses all the time. Yet, over the years it has also been one of my greatest weaknesses, one that I have had to pray about continually.

These things keep us dependent on God and not ourselves. In order to succeed at being ourselves, we must understand how to receive grace, favor and mercy. We cannot receive something if we do not even understand what it is. It is vitally important to remember that grace is God's undeserved favor which we receive through our faith. It leaves us thankful and living our lives with an "attitude of gratitude."

BELIEVE IN THE FAVOR OF GOD

> *But the Lord was with Joseph, and showed him mercy and loving-kindness and gave him favor in the sight of the warden of the prison.*
> *Genesis 39:21*

There are many people spoken of in the Bible who received favor. Since God is no respecter of persons (Acts 10:34), we can believe for and receive favor in our daily lives.

In Genesis 39 we read how Joseph was unjustly accused and imprisoned. But the Lord was with him and showed him mercy and grace. He gave him favor in the eyes of the prison warden, who put Joseph in charge of everything that went on there. In fact, the warden looked on Joseph so favorably that he paid no attention to what

Joseph did, and the Lord caused his efforts to prosper even in that dismal situation.

Favor is available to us also, but like many other good things in life, just because something is available to us does not mean that we will ever partake of it. The Lord makes many things available to us that we never receive and enjoy because we never activate our faith in that area.

I needed a lot of favor to get to where I am today in ministry. I believe I have succeeded at being myself, the person God originally intended me to be, but it could never have happened without favor. For example, when we began our television ministry in 1993 practically nobody even knew Joyce Meyer existed. I knew we would need a lot of favor from God if we were to get on quality television stations around the world. I knew God had to open doors for us. I was willing to walk through them boldly, but He had to open them and not only give me favor with television station owners and managers, but also with television audiences.

I am a very bold, straightforward, tell-it-like-I-see-it woman. Many people don't handle that type of personality very well, so I knew I needed favor. I needed God to show people my heart and help them believe that I wanted to help them.

I think we all have some personality quirks that can turn people off, so praying for favor is a wise thing to do. When God gives us favor, people favor us — and often for no reason they can even explain. If three people applied for the same position and were all equally qualified, the one living under the favor of God would get it.

Favor is actually a part of grace. In the English New Testament the word *grace* and the word *favor* are both translated from the same Greek word *charis*.[1] So the grace of God is the favor of God. And the favor of God is the grace of God — that which causes things to happen in our life that need to happen, through the channel of our faith — the power of God doing something for us that we can neither earn nor deserve.

When we say to someone, "Can you do me a favor?" we are asking that person to do something for us that we have neither earned nor paid for. We are depending on that individual's goodness to manifest in the form of a blessing, even though there is no natural reason for it to be given.

Esther, Daniel and the Hebrew children, Ruth and even Jesus Himself received favor from God that caused them to be accepted instead of rejected in specific situations. They may have been rejected in some areas, but they were accepted regarding the thing God had sent them to do.

I do not experience total acceptance and favor everywhere I go, and neither does anyone else. But I have experienced great favor as far as people receiving my teaching ministry. I have been invited to speak in some of the finest conferences in the world today, alongside great men and women of God whom I respect and admire. I know it is a manifestation of the favor of God, and I appreciate it.

Esther needed favor with the king. She was selected by God to bring deliverance to her people who were in danger. She stepped out in faith and went into a place that was hard for her in the natural. God gave her the favor she was believing for, and she fulfilled the call on her life.

Ruth was a Moabite, so there was no way for her to be accepted by the Israelites without favor from God because the Moabites were idolaters. God gave her that favor because she loved and trusted Him. She did nothing special to deserve it, but her heart was right before God. Due to favor she married Boaz, *a man of great wealth* (Ruth 2:1 NKJV), and their ancestral line brought forth David from whom Jesus Himself was descended.

I think we can see that favor is very valuable and necessary in order to succeed at being all God intends us to be. We should pray for supernatural favor on a regular basis and expect to receive it. To be very honest, it is just plain fun to watch God favor us in certain situations.

I know you have had times of receiving favor, and I am sure you enjoyed it very much. I am encouraging you to release your faith in this area in a greater way than ever before. Don't be afraid to ask God to give you favor.

I believe there are many things God would do for us, if we would be bold enough to ask. Boldness in prayer cannot be obtained without an understanding of mercy. We all make mistakes, and our reward should be punishment, not favor. That is exactly why boldness is required to go before the Lord and ask first for forgiveness and then for mercy. Forgiveness takes care of our sin, and mercy blesses us even though we don't deserve it. Forgiveness is actually a manifestation of God's mercy. He forgives us because He is merciful and long-suffering.

MERCY! MERCY! MERCY!

> *It is because of the Lord's mercy and loving-kindness that we are not consumed, because His [tender] compassions fail not. They are new every morning; great and abundant is Your stability and faithfulness.*
> *Lamentations 3:22,23*

I frequently say, "It's a good thing God's mercy is new every morning, because I have used up all of yesterday's supply!"

Mercy is another word that is in close relationship and even interchangeable to a degree with *grace* and *favor*. In Noah Webster's 1828 *American Dictionary of the English Language* he defines *mercy* as:

"That benevolence, mildness or tenderness of heart which disposes a person to overlook injuries, or to treat an offender better than he deserves; the disposition that tempers justice, and induces an injured person to forgive trespasses and injuries, and to forbear punishment, or inflict less than law or justice will warrant. In this sense, there is perhaps no word in our language precisely synonymous with *mercy*. That which comes nearest to it is *grace*. It implies benevolence, tenderness, mildness, pity or compassion, and clemency, but exercised only towards offenders. *Mercy* is a distinguishing attribute of the Supreme Being."[2]

I don't know about you, but I am extremely happy about God's mercy. I cannot possibly imagine where I would be today if it were not for it. I know for sure I would not be anywhere pleasant.

We all deserve punishment, but instead God gives us mercy. What an awesome God we serve! The psalms are filled with references to His mercy. Psalm 107:1 is an example: *O give thanks to the Lord, for He is good; for His mercy and loving-kindness endure forever!*

David was a man who loved God very much, yet he made serious mistakes. His passions gained the mastery over him and caused him to commit adultery and have a man murdered. I believe David talked so much about the mercy of God because he had experienced it firsthand in his life and ministry.

God's mercy forgives and restores, and only a person like David who has been honest in his evaluation of himself can truly say, *O give thanks to the Lord, for He is good; for His mercy and loving-kindness endure forever!*

MERCY AND MINISTRY

But Paul selected Silas and set out, being commended by the brethren to the grace (the favor and mercy) of the Lord.
And he passed through Syria and Cilicia, establishing and strengthening the churches.
Acts 15:40,41

It is obvious from this Scripture that believers in the early Church knew their success in ministry was dependent upon God's grace, favor and mercy. We would do well to remember that fact in our own ministries. We make much greater progress depending on His grace, favor and mercy than we ever do depending on our own good works or efforts to *deserve* His help.

Our ministries do not grow and prosper due to our goodness, but to God's. He is all goodness, while we must say with Paul in Romans 7:18, *...I know that nothing good dwells within me, that is, in my flesh....*

As ministers of the Gospel of Jesus Christ, it is imperative that we be merciful, but it is impossible for us to be merciful if we have not learned our own need for mercy and practiced receiving it from the Lord. It is our own weaknesses and failures that cause us to have compassion on the weak and erring.

I am sure that if I were perfect I would expect everyone else to be perfect also. When I have a memory lapse concerning my own faults, I sometimes find myself being too harsh with others. At such times, God is obliged to remind me of my own frailties once again. He has a way of hiding in the shadows and allowing us to get into enough trouble to keep us humble and therefore useable. He stands back and allows our weaknesses to surface so we must trust Him and not ourselves.

As evidence, please consider this passage written by the great Apostle Paul in 2 Corinthians:

> For we do not want you to be uninformed, brethren, about the affliction and oppressing distress which befell us in [the province of] Asia, how we were so utterly and unbearably weighed down and crushed that we despaired even of life [itself].
> Indeed, we felt within ourselves that we had received the [very] sentence of death, but that was to keep us from trusting

in and depending on ourselves instead of on God Who raises
the dead.
2 Corinthians 1:8,9

Jesus Himself gave instruction concerning the importance of being merciful, when He told the religious leaders of His day, *Go and learn what this means: I desire mercy [that is, readiness to help those in trouble] and not sacrifice and sacrificial victims. For I came not to call and invite [to repentance] the righteous (those who are upright and in right standing with God), but sinners (the erring ones and all those not free from sin)* (Matthew 9:13).

Under the Old Covenant when people sinned, they had to make sacrifices to atone for their sins. In this passage in Matthew's Gospel, Jesus was introducing the New Covenant, which includes freedom from the need to sacrifice. Jesus became the perfect and final sacrifice for all those who would believe, and He now instructs us to receive mercy from Him for our failures and to give mercy to others who fail.

This does not mean there is no correction or punishment for sin, but God always tries to draw us into righteousness through His love and mercy before dealing more harshly with us. We can understand this principle better when we think of our own children.

I have said many times: "I give my children my word first. If they listen, all is well. If they don't listen and get into trouble, I will show mercy and tell them again and sometimes again and again. But eventually if they don't pay heed to my word, I will touch their circumstances." I don't do that because I want to, but because I have to in order to help them.

It pays not to be stubborn. Repenting and receiving God's mercy is much better than enduring His chastisement.

I have learned to take this same approach with our employees and others over whom I have authority. I always show mercy first and quite frequently for an extended period of time, but I know in my spirit when it is time to deal with issues more sternly.

Some people cannot appreciate the mercy of God until they have experienced a bit of His wrath. God is never wrathful against His people; His wrath is always against the sin in their lives. He hates sin, and we must learn to hate it also.

Like God, we must hate sin, but love the sinner.

You may have a call into full-time ministry, or you may be a lay person who desires to minister to others in your everyday life. If so, I cannot stress enough how important it is that you learn how to give and receive mercy. Remember, you cannot give away something you don't have in you.

If we do not receive God's mercy for our failures, we will not have any to give to others when they fail us and disappoint us. We cannot lead people into powerful relationships with the Lord through harshness, hardness, rigidity and legalism. We must show them that the God we serve is merciful, patient and long-suffering.

God is love, and all of these things we are discussing are facets of His love. Walking in love is the high call on the life of every believer. There is no possibility of true ministry without walking in love.

No one can have a powerful ministry who does not display the love of God, nor can one put faith in something unknown. God's grace, favor and mercy were available to me all of my life, but I did not start receiving them until I was more than forty years old. I could not receive them because I knew nothing of them and did not even believe in them.

I pray that this chapter has given you a better understanding of the words *receive, grace, favor* and *mercy*. Properly understood, they will release power into your life and ministry.

9

BELIEVING AND RECEIVING

9
BELIEVING AND RECEIVING

In a certain sense the word *receive* is synonymous with the word *believe*. We cannot receive something if we don't believe in it.

...all things can be (are possible) to him who believes!
MARK 9:23

In the spiritual realm, when you and I believe something, we receive it into our heart. If a physical manifestation is needed, it will come after we have believed — not before. In the world, we are taught to believe what we see. In God's Kingdom, we must learn to believe first, and then we will see manifested what we have believed (received, admitted in our heart).[1]

I know from Scripture that God has a good plan for each of our lives. I began to aggressively believe that several years ago, and I am now experiencing it. The good plan for me was available all along, but for most of my life I did not believe it; therefore, I could not receive it.

The Lord is willing to take every negative thing that has happened to us and turn it into something positive, if we will only believe.

BELIEVING IS RECEIVING! ————————————————

The Spirit of the Lord God is upon me, because the Lord has anointed and qualified me to preach the Gospel of good tidings to the meek, the poor, and afflicted; He has sent me to bind up and heal the brokenhearted, to proclaim liberty to the [physical and spiritual] captives and the opening of the prison and of the eyes to those who are bound,
To proclaim the acceptable year of the Lord [the year of His favor] and the day of vengeance of our God, to comfort all who mourn,

To grant [consolation and joy] to those who mourn in Zion
— to give them an ornament (a garland or diadem) of beauty
instead of ashes, the oil of joy instead of mourning, the
garment [expressive] of praise instead of a heavy, burdened,
and failing spirit — that they may be called oaks of right-
eousness [lofty, strong, and magnificent, distinguished for
uprightness, justice, and right standing with God], the plant-
ing of the Lord, that He may be glorified.
Isaiah 61:1-3

Through the years I have hung onto Scriptures like the one above as well as others and have found from experience that believing God's Word consistently will eventually turn circumstances from negative to positive. A lot of negative things have happened to me, and Satan used them to sour my attitude toward life and people. I was trapped in my past, because I did not believe I had a future. As soon as I believed, I was released from the past and began making progress toward the good thing God had in mind for me. It did not all come to me immediately in manifested form, but believing gave me renewed hope that kept me going from day to day. Slowly but surely I began to see changes take place in my life, and each change encouraged me to believe more.

Believing is the key to receiving from God!

No matter what has happened to you in the past, if you believe, you can receive the good future that is set aside for you in Jesus Christ Who came to do the will of His Father in heaven.

CHRIST IN YOU, THE HOPE OF GLORY

The mystery of which was hidden for ages and generations
[from angels and men], but is now revealed to His holy people
(the saints),
To whom God was pleased to make known how great for
the Gentiles are the riches of the glory of this mystery, which

is Christ within and among you, the Hope of [realizing
the] glory.
Colossians 1:26,27

You and I can only realize and experience the glory of God in our lives because of Christ in us. He is our hope of seeing better things.

The glory of God is His manifested excellence. As the children of God, we have a blood-bought right to experience the best God has planned for us. Satan furiously fights the plan of God in each of our lives, and his primary weapon is deception. When we are deceived, we believe something that is not true. Even though it is not true, it seems true for us because that is what we believe.

When we look at ourselves and our own ability, we feel defeated, but remembering that Christ in us is our hope of realizing the glory. It keeps us encouraged enough to press on toward better things. We limit ourselves when we look to ourselves alone and fail to see Jesus.

In John 11:40 Jesus said to Martha, ...*Did I not tell you and promise you that if you would believe and rely on Me, you would see the glory of God?* The Lord has destined His Church for glory. He is coming back for a glorious Church. (Ephesians 5:27.) We can be excellent people with excellent attitudes, excellent thoughts and excellent words. God's glory can be manifested in us and on us, but only as we believe it is possible.

God is looking for someone who will believe and receive. Start expecting more of His glory in your life. He is waiting to manifest His glory — to you and through you!

RECEIVING GOD'S STRENGTH

No man shall be able to stand before you all the days of your life. As I was with Moses, so I will be with you; I will not fail you or forsake you.
Joshua 1:5

I often think of Joshua and how he must have felt when God told him that he was to take Moses' place and lead the Israelites into the Promised Land. Moses was an amazing leader. Who would want to try to fill his shoes?

God told Joshua that he would succeed, not because of anything he had in the natural, but because He was with him. Moses was successful only because God was with him. God told Joshua that the same thing would hold true for him if he believed. God kept encouraging Joshua to be strong and confident, to take courage and not be afraid. In other words, He kept telling him to *believe!*

God asks you and me to put our faith in Him and to believe that we can do whatever He asks us to do. He is mighty to uphold us and make us stand. He will support us and keep us from failing.

God's strength is readily available to us. We receive it through believing in it, and the promise God has made to give it to us. If we believe we are weak, then we will only manifest weakness, but the Bible says, *...let the weak say, I am strong...* (Joel 3:10). When we can say we are strong with a heart of conviction, even though we are weak in ourselves, the Lord will be strong in us — we will experience victory in our lives!

BELIEVERS ARE SUPPOSED TO BELIEVE!

I have strength for all things in Christ Who empowers me [I am ready for anything and equal to anything through Him Who infuses inner strength into me; I am self-sufficient in Christ's sufficiency].
Philippians 4:13

I love Philippians 4:13. It has encouraged me many times in life. I have learned to believe that I am ready for anything that comes my way through Christ, Who gives me the strength when I need it.

Just because we don't *feel strong* when we think about a situation does not mean that we won't *be strong* when we need to be. God's strength comes to us by His grace, through our faith, but He rarely gives us the strength we need before we actually need it. In this way we must trust Him, which is our part. God asks us to trust Him, and as we do, He does the part we cannot do.

When we awake on any morning, we don't know for certain what may happen to us that day. We all hope for easy days in which all of our desires are being met, yet we know from experience that is not always the case. We live in a real world, with real problems. Our enemy, the devil, is real, and he is working through everyone he possibly can to bring discouragement, fear and failure to us because we belong to God and put our trust in Him.

GOD IS OUR REFUGE AND OUR FORTRESS ——————

> *I will say of the Lord, He is my Refuge and my Fortress, my God; on Him I lean and rely, and in Him I [confidently] trust!...*
> *You shall not be afraid of the terror of the night, nor of the arrow (the evil plots and slanders of the wicked) that flies by day,*
> *Nor of the pestilence that stalks in darkness, nor of the destruction and sudden death that surprise and lay waste at noonday.*
> *Psalm 91:2,5,6*

Psalm 91 teaches us that through trusting God we don't have to be afraid of the devil's sudden surprises that stalk us. No matter what may come our way, we should *believe right now* that when it arrives we will be able. If we trust God, He will make us strong, and we will not be defeated.

151

We need to remember that we are ready for anything, equal to anything, through Christ Who infuses inner strength into us. Inner strength is actually more valuable than outer strength; we need to stand up on the inside and refuse to believe the lies of Satan.

Paul prayed for the Church at Ephesus to be strengthened with all might and power in the inner man. (Ephesians 3:16 KJV.) He knew if they stayed strong inwardly, they would be able to handle anything that came against them outwardly and be able to do whatever they needed to do.

WAIT FOR THE LORD

> *But those who wait for the Lord [who expect, look for, and hope in Him] shall change and renew their strength and power; they shall lift their wings and mount up [close to God] as eagles [mount up to the sun]; they shall run and not be weary, they shall walk and not faint or become tired.*
> *Isaiah 40:31*

Isaiah teaches us to wait for the Lord when we know our strength needs to be renewed. Waiting for God means spending time with Him in His Word and His Presence.

There are certain people we can draw strength from just by being around them. Their very presence, the way they talk and approach life, seems to make us feel better when we are discouraged or feeling down in any way. Likewise, there are others who can always make us feel worse. They have a way of putting a negative edge onto everything.

When you and I need to be strengthened, we should spend time with God and with people filled with His Spirit. Spending time in God's Presence is like sitting in a room filled with sweet-smelling perfume. If we sit there long enough, we take the fragrance with us when we leave. It will be in our clothing, in our hair and even in our very skin.

Moses was a man of prayer, he spent a great deal of time fellowshipping with and talking to God. He knew that if God did not help him, he would fail miserably. Because of Moses' faithfulness to seek God, he was given an assuring message: *And the Lord said, My Presence shall go with you, and I will give you rest* (Exodus 33:14).

Moses had to face many hostile enemies as well as try to lead God's people across the wilderness into the Promised Land. We cannot even imagine the magnitude of the task at hand. There were millions of Israelites — they were murmuring, complaining and finding fault with Moses most of the time. This was an ideal situation for Moses to lose his peace, yet God told him, "My Presence will go with you, and I will give you rest." Moses believed God, and therefore received God's promise. I am sure there were times when his faith got stretched, times when it did not look or feel as if God was with Him.

According to Hebrews 11:1, faith is the evidence of things hoped for but not seen, the conviction of their reality. It is still absolutely amazing to me how fast my attitude can change from negative to positive simply by an adjustment in what I am believing.

We can receive from Satan by believing what he says, or we can receive from God by believing His Word. We all believe something, it may as well be something good.

Always remember that *it does not cost anything to believe!* Try it, you will find your life changing in an amazing way.

DO YOU NEED A CHECKUP FROM THE NECK UP?

Blessed (happy, fortunate, to be envied) is the man whose strength is in You, in whose heart are the highways to Zion.

Passing through the Valley of Weeping (Baca), they make it a place of springs; the early rain also fills [the pools] with blessings. They go from strength to strength [increasing in victorious power]; each of them appears before God in Zion.
Psalm 84:5–7

When our strength is in God, even the difficult places in life can be turned into blessings. That's why we need to constantly keep our minds and hearts focused on Him and not on our circumstances.

It is wise to occasionally take an inventory of our thought life. It may be that we have lost our joy and are failing to realize why.

I have discovered that when I am unhappy I have a temptation to start blaming my unhappiness on some circumstance or person in my life who is not giving me what I feel I need. That type of wrong thinking can cause us to go around the same mountain again and again, failing to make any progress toward enjoying God's promises. (Deuteronomy 2:3.)

Most of the time when I am unhappy, it is because of some wrong thinking on my part. Even if I have negative circumstances, I can stay happy by having right thoughts toward them. If people are not giving me what I need, I can either be angry with them or I can look to God to meet my need.

Satan wants us to *think* that nothing will ever change, that things will only get worse. He wants us to inventory every disappointing thing that has ever happened in our lives and *think* about how mistreated we have been. We will absolutely never fulfill our destinies and succeed at being all God has planned for us if we don't think properly.

Don't think according to the past, think according to the Word of God.

What you believe determines whether you will receive the manifestation of fullness in your life.

Far too many people testify to emptiness and dryness in their lives.

God has satisfaction, fullness and completeness in mind for us. I never felt satisfied or complete in my life until I was doing what God had ordained for me to do. Fullness only comes through being in the center of God's will. If you and I don't get into agreement with God through right believing, we will never make any progress toward the end fulfillment of our destinies.

YOU'VE GOT TO HAVE A DREAM!

> *Where there is no vision [no redemptive revelation of God], the people perish; but he who keeps the law [of God, which includes that of man] — blessed (happy, fortunate, and enviable) is he.*
> *Proverbs 29:18*

Those with a sad past need to be able to believe in a bright future. The writer of Proverbs says that where there is no vision, people perish.

A vision is something we see in our mind, "a mental sight" as one definition puts it. It may be something God plants in us supernaturally or something we see on purpose. It involves the way we think about ourselves, our past and our future. Remember what I said earlier — *it does not cost anything to believe.*

Some people are afraid to believe. They think they may be setting themselves up for disappointment. They have not realized they will be perpetually disappointed if they don't believe.

I feel that if I believe for a lot and even get half of it, I am better off than I would be to believe for nothing and get all of it.

I am challenging you to start believing good things. Believe you can do whatever you need to do in life through Christ. Don't have a "give up easy" attitude. Let your faith soar. Be creative with your thoughts. Take an inventory: what have you been believing lately? An honest answer may help you understand why you have not been receiving what you have wanted to receive.

10

STANDING UP
ON THE INSIDE

10
STANDING UP
ON THE INSIDE

I once heard the story of a little boy attending church with his mother, who kept standing up at the wrong time. His mother repeatedly told him to sit down, and finally she got very strong

I have fought the good fight, I have finished the race, I have kept the faith. 2 TIMOTHY 4:7 NKJV

with him about it, telling him emphatically, "Sit down now, or you will be in trouble when we go home!" The little boy looked at her and said, "I'll sit down, but I'm still going to be standing up on the inside."

It seems to me that someone in life is always trying to get us to sit down. They tell us not to make waves, not to be heard or noticed. They want us to simply go along with the program others have designed and forget about what we want personally.

Through the years, many people tried to hold me back from the call on my life. There were those who did not understand what I was doing and why I was doing it, so they judged me falsely. At times their criticism and judgment made me want to "sit down" and forget about my vision from God. There were others who were embarrassed by having a "lady preacher" for a friend or relative; they wanted me to "sit down" so their reputation would not be affected adversely. Many rejected me, and the pain of their rejection tempted me to "sit down" and quietly go along with the group.

But I had a big God standing up on the inside of me, and "sitting down" was not an option to me. He caused me to stand up on the inside and be determined to go forward no matter what others thought, said or did. It was not always easy, but I learned from my experience that being frustrated and unfulfilled due to being out of the will of God is more difficult than pressing through all the opposition.

Standing up on the inside does not mean being rebellious or having an aggressive attitude toward those who don't understand us. It means having a quiet inner confidence that takes us through to the finish line. It is knowing inside that despite what is going on the outside, everything is going to be all right because God is on the scene, and when He is present nothing is impossible.

In order to succeed at being ourselves, we must be faithful to God all the way to the end. We can never quit or give up.

I believe there are probably very few people who completely succeed at being all they can be. The opposition is too great. It is easy to get defeated. However, those who are determined to remain standing on the inside no matter what happens will cross the finish line! They will be able to say with Jesus, "Father, glorify me now, for I have completed the work You have given me to do." (John 17:4,5.)

TWO THINGS THAT INTERRUPT FAITH

> But Christ (the Messiah) was faithful over His [own Father's] house as a Son [and Master of it]. And it is we who are [now members] of this house, **if** we hold fast and firm to the end our joyful and exultant confidence and sense of triumph in our hope [in Christ].
> Hebrews 3:6

I emphasized the word *if* in this passage because often we don't like to pay attention to the ifs and buts in the Bible. In Scriptures like this one, we see what God will do, *if* we will do what we are supposed to do.

You and I have the awesome privilege of being members of the Father's house, *if* we remain firm in faith until the end. Going to the altar and praying a sinner's prayer is only the beginning of our walk with Him; we must follow through and continue in faith — we must keep believing in Him!

Confidence and faith are virtually synonymous; sometimes they can be interchanged without losing the context of what is being said at all. I could give a long fancy definition of faith, but suffice it to say that faith is confidence in God. In simple terms, faith is knowing that if God has said He will do something, He will do it. Even if it doesn't look like He is doing it right now, it will come to pass in His timing, *if* we will remain confident in Him.

The only two things that can interrupt faith are 1) the manifestation of what is believed or 2) the manifestation of doubt and unbelief. Once we receive the manifestation of what we have been believing for, we no longer need faith, so it ceases in that case. In the same way, the manifestation of doubt and unbelief — that is, receiving the lies of Satan and believing them — interrupts faith, so that it ceases to exist.

That is why our faith must continue, even when it seems that everything and everyone is against us. In Christ, we can remain standing firm on the inside because we know that our real life is in us, not in the people or circumstances around us.

PUT CONFIDENCE IN GOD, NOT IN FLESH

For we [Christians] are the true circumcision, who worship God in spirit and by the Spirit of God and exult and glory and pride ourselves in Jesus Christ, and put no confidence or dependence [on what we are] in the flesh and on outward privileges and physical advantages and external appearances.
Philippians 3:3

Confidence in God is a totally different thing from self-confidence. As I have already mentioned, we believers are to put no confidence in the flesh. In my ministry, I work to destroy people's self-confidence and to get them to the point that their confidence is in Christ and Him alone. God opposes our independent attitude, and He will aggressively deal with us until all of it is removed.

We should have a sense of inward triumph, but it can only be found in Christ.

TRIUMPH IN CHRIST

But thanks be to God, Who in Christ always leads us in triumph [as trophies of Christ's victory] and through us spreads and makes evident the fragrance of the knowledge of God everywhere.
2 Corinthians 2:14

As we saw in Chapter 5, according to Romans 8:37 we are more than conquerors in Christ. I believe we are more than conquerors when we know we already have the victory before the trouble ever starts. That kind of confidence is an inward assurance, not in ourselves, but in the God Who indwells us.

My husband Dave is not a man who is afraid of circumstances. They don't frighten him or cause him to change his position at all. He has a quiet confidence that no matter what happens, God will take care of it *if* we will keep our trust in Him. Dave definitely walks with this sense of inward triumph, a more-than-a-conqueror attitude. He is definitely a man who remains standing on the inside no matter what comes against him on the outside.

Over the years, I have watched him in many different situations, and he has handled them all the same way. He casts his care on God and keeps trusting and believing that all things work together for good to those who love God and are called according to His purpose. (Romans 8:28 KJV.) When he tries to do something and it does not work out, when someone rejects him, when someone judges or criticizes our ministry, when we are in financial need, or even when he and

I are struggling in our personal relationship, he always maintains that quiet confidence that in the end everything will work out all right.

Recently, I talked with a friend who spent much of her life worrying about her two children. One married a few years ago and has a great life, and the other is scheduled to be married soon to a wonderful man. I remarked to her how much time we waste worrying about our children, and how it really is wasted energy. I noted how things usually work out in the end and how worrying only contributes to the problem; it does not provide the answer.

In my earlier life, I went through the same thing this mother experienced. I worried about certain issues with each of my children while they were young. Now they are grown, and all the things I worried about have worked out.

As I have explained, I worried about my oldest daughter, Laura, because she did not like school and got mediocre grades. She was an undisciplined teenager — undisciplined with her personal belongings and her money. She wanted to get married young and have children, and I felt she was not even taking care of herself, let alone prepared to have a family. When she got married at age nineteen, I had nagged her so much that our relationship was anything but good. Dave had told me repeatedly, "Joyce, Laura will turn out fine. She will make it."

Now Laura is in her thirties and is so well organized that she helps keep me organized. Her marriage is great, she has two wonderful children and all is well. She went through some rough times learning some of the lessons she needed to learn after she was away from home, but learning things the hard way is often the best way — we usually never forget what we have learned by experience.

While I was falling apart on the inside, Dave was standing up on the inside and refusing to let circumstances rule him. I believe we are more than conquerors when we don't fear trouble. None of us have nice little lives that are totally trouble free — if we bow down to fear there will always be something to fear.

STEP OUT AND FIND OUT

> ..."Launch out into the deep and let down your nets for
> a catch."
> Luke 5:4 NKJV

The only way we ever reach our final destination and succeed at being our true selves is to take many, many steps of faith. Stepping out into the unknown — into something we have never done before — can leave us shaking in our boots.

Because of feelings of fear, many people never "step out," therefore they never "find out" what they are capable of.

I believe we are very close to the time when Jesus will return for His Church, and I don't think He has time to spend months and months convincing each of us to obey when He wants us to step out into something. I believe the more we progress into what we call "the last days," the more God is going to require radical steps of obedience.

Many people are missing the will of God for their lives because they are "playing it safe." I don't want to come to the end of my life and say, "I was safe, but I'm sorry."

The world has a little saying: "Better safe than sorry." I am not sure that always works in God's economy. If I had tried to be safe all the time, I am sure I would not be where I am today. I would never have sown the seeds of obedience in my life that have produced the harvest I now enjoy in my ministry and in many other areas of my life.

I am not suggesting we all start doing a bunch of foolish things that are unwise, but I know for a fact that not everything God wants us to do makes sense to the natural mind. You and I must learn to be led by discernment in the inner man (the spirit) and not by our own carnal minds, or what other people suggest to us. When we step out, we should do all we can to be sure it is the voice of God to which we are responding in faith and obedience and not just some wild thought we have picked up out of the atmosphere where it was placed by Satan to try to lure us into destruction.

Dave and I have found that the best policy is "one step at a time." When we have something on our hearts, we pray awhile and wait awhile. If it stays in our hearts, we take a step. If it works, and we see that God is anointing it, we take another step.

People who get into serious trouble usually don't do so in one big jump; more often it is the result of many wrong steps. God has warned them along the way and tried to keep them out of trouble, but they have pressed on in the flesh (following their own carnal desires), trying to make what they want to be God's will.

Here is a good example of the right way to step out in faith. When Dave and I believed God was telling us to go on television, we did not contract with four hundred stations at the beginning. First, we contacted our partners and asked them to invest in the equipment we needed, *if* they felt God was leading them to do so. We knew that if God was indeed telling us to go on television, then He would also tell others to help us.

When all the money we needed came in, we took another step. We went on a handful of stations and went back to our partners in the ministry, asking them to help us again by committing a certain amount of money that would enable us to pay the bills for air time the first few months while our program was getting established. Once again they responded with what we needed, and so we pressed forward.

Over the years we have added stations as we have been able to pay for the ones we are already on. We would not have continued to add stations if the ones we were on were not paying for themselves.

STANDING UP ON THE INSIDE

As of this writing I have thirty-three published books on the market. Had I written one or two and sold none I would not have continued to write more.

Some people get into trouble simply because they are unable to admit they made a mistake and find a new direction. It is very difficult to get into serious trouble stepping out one step at a time. But those who won't step out are already in serious trouble because they will never accomplish anything in life.

Another safety factor we have followed is being sure our hearts are right concerning the thing we are doing. We have to be sure we have pure motives and are doing it solely because we believe it is God's will.

Some people get into trouble because they do what other people think they should do. Others do things to get attention or to imitate what they see someone else doing.

Many ministers were on television a long time before I was. As a matter of fact, I can remember many people saying to me, "Why don't you go on television, Joyce?" or "Joyce, don't you want to be on television?" To be honest, I did not want to be on television. I didn't want the financial responsibility. I had a very successful radio ministry, and I wanted to stay in the "safe zone." But when God said, "I want you to go on television," He also filled my heart with desire.

Other people can want things for us, but we must want them ourselves or we will never press through the difficulties that come with giving birth to a new thing.

I wanted to make sure my motive was right for going on television. God is not looking for people who want to be stars — He is looking for people who want to help others. It is always good to take some time to examine our motives. Being honest with ourselves about motives can save us many failures.

Recently we have been greatly encouraged by several people to advertise our conferences in a greater way. While it is true that people won't come if they don't know we are there, it is also true that we could waste a lot of money doing things the world's way that won't necessarily work in the Kingdom of God.

God has His own ways!

Some of the things suggested to us we felt very good about, and others we did not. I don't feel it is my job to "sell myself." It is my job to obey God, love people, be where I believe the Lord wants me to be and, after having done my part to advertise properly, trust Him to speak to people to come. I did not feel I could do some of the things people were suggesting and do them with right motives, so I decided not to even try. I believe God will honor that decision and give the increase we desire.

RADICAL OBEDIENCE OFTEN REQUIRES SACRIFICE ──────

> *...Truly I tell you, there is no one who has given up and left house or brothers or sisters or mother or father or children or lands for My sake and for the Gospel's*
> *Who will not receive a hundred times as much now in this time — houses and brothers and sisters and mothers and children and lands, with persecutions — and in the age to come, eternal life.*
> *Mark 10:29,30*

Life In The Word maintains an office in Australia, and we needed two couples from our ministry to go there and manage that branch. In order to move there, the couples basically had to give up everything they had and start over. It would have been too expensive to ship a lot of personal belongings that far.

Two couples did take a step of obedience as they felt God speaking to their hearts that they were the ones to go. They stepped out, but in order to do so they had to make huge personal sacrifices. They had to sell their cars and furniture, leave behind family and friends and separate themselves from churches in which they were deeply rooted. They had to leave everything and everyone they loved in order to obey God and move to a faraway place. Obviously, despite their love of God and their desire to do His will, it was a difficult transition.

When we go to a new place, we often experience loneliness, a feeling that everything and everyone around us is strange. We don't feel comfortable or "at home." But that kind of radical obedience pays great dividends in the personal happiness and contentment that come from knowing we are in the will of God, and in the material blessings that God provides for us in accordance with the promises found in His Word.

THE RIGHTEOUS WILL SUFFER PERSECUTION ─────────

> *Indeed all who delight in piety and are determined to live a devoted and godly life in Christ Jesus will meet with persecution [will be made to suffer because of their religious stand].*
> *2 Timothy 3:12*

The Word of God tells us that we will have persecution. In *Vine's Complete Expository Dictionary of Old and New Testament Words,* the Greek word translated *persecute* is partially defined as "to put to flight, drive away."[1] Satan brings opposition, trouble, trials and tribulations in the hope of driving us away. If we intend to succeed at being ourselves and being all God wants us to be, we must be prepared to stand strong in times of persecution.

If we will keep standing up on the inside, God will take care of the outside.

The Charismatic Church has not been real comfortable with the word *sacrifice* — but it is in the Bible. In Mark 8:34, Jesus said, in essence, "If you want to follow Me, you will have to give up your self-life to do so."

THE REQUIREMENT AND REWARD OF SACRIFICE————

Now [in Haran] the Lord said to Abram, Go for yourself
[for your own advantage] away from your country, from
your relatives and your father's house, to the land that I will
show you.
And I will make of you a great nation, and I will bless you
[with abundant increase of favors] and make your name
famous and distinguished, and you will be a blessing
[dispensing good to others].
Genesis 12:1,2

We have seen that Abram (later renamed Abraham) had to make a sacrifice when God told him to leave his father's house and go to the place He would show him at a later time. God required some radical obedience on the part of Abram, but He also made him a radical promise.

When we think of sacrifice, we must always remember that what we sow as a seed, God uses to bring a harvest. When we are called upon to make a sacrifice, we should not feel deprived, but privileged. Jesus sacrificed His very life for us, and we are to follow in His footsteps. (1 Peter 2:21.)

We don't have to be comfortable all the time. In America and many other parts of the world, God's people are addicted to "comfort and ease." It is time to shake ourselves into reality and start doing what He asks us to do, no matter what the cost.

We cannot expect radical harvest in our lives if we sow seeds of disobedience. True to God's promise, Abraham went on to be the father of many nations and the father of the Old Covenant. Considering the number of people on the earth at that time, I would say that was quite an honor for Abraham.

There are some very radical examples in the Bible of things people did to obey God. It was radical of Esther to walk away from whatever plans she had for her life and put everything on the line when she went before the king without being summoned. Her motive was right, and she did it in obedience; therefore, God gave her favor, and she was instrumental in saving her nation from disaster.

It was radical of Daniel to continue praying three times a day with his windows open after being warned he would be placed into the lions' den if he did so. He took a radical step of obedience and ended up outlasting three kings, all of whom promoted him.

It was radical of the Apostle Paul to come back among the same people he had been persecuting and preach the Gospel to them. What if they attacked him? He became the bond-slave of Jesus Christ and in his own words, *a prisoner for His sake* (2 Timothy 1:8). Paul was given approximately two-thirds of the New Testament by direct revelation from God. We see how God honored his steps of radical obedience and personal sacrifice. When God called him, he was a very respected Pharisee enjoying prestige and personal comfort. His steps of obedience often left him hungry, hunted, cold, beaten, and in prison — but he knew the secret of standing up on the inside, and his quiet confidence in God brought him all the way through to the end of the journey.

Paul made a powerful statement when he said, *...none of these things move me; neither do I esteem my life dear to myself, if only I may finish my course with joy...* (Acts 20:24). That should be our testimony as well, as we are told in God's Word.

FINISH WHAT YOU START

> *For we have become fellows with Christ (the Messiah) and share in all He has for us, if only we hold our first newborn confidence and original assured expectation [in virtue of which we are believers] firm and unshaken to the end.*
> *Hebrews 3:14*

Do not, therefore, fling away your fearless confidence, for it carries a great and glorious compensation of reward.
Hebrews 10:35

But we do [strongly and earnestly] desire for each of you to show the same diligence and sincerity [all the way through] in realizing and enjoying the full assurance and development of [your] hope until the end.
Hebrews 6:11

All of the Scriptures above should be meditated upon and taken very seriously. God is not interested in our starting things that we never finish. It is easy to begin, but it takes great courage to finish. In the beginning of a new thing we get all excited. We have a lot of emotions (ours and everyone else's) to support us. When the emotions wear off and all that is left is a lot of hard work and the need for extreme patience, we find out who really has what it takes to truly succeed.

In God's mind we are never successful if we stop somewhere along the way. He wants us to finish our course and do it with joy!

If you have been tempted even recently to give up — don't! If you don't finish the thing you are currently involved in, you will face the same challenges in the next thing you start.

Some people spend all their lives starting new things and never finishing anything. Let us make a decision that we will be more than a statistic that never reached its full potential.

We can start out in faith, but we are supposed to live from faith to faith. (Romans 1:17.) In other words, there are many plateaus along the way that require greater faith than the last one we reached. God is always taking us up — never back and never down! He is always calling us up higher. We must leave the lower life and press on toward the high places. We must live from faith to faith, not from faith to doubt to unbelief and then back to a little faith.

From Faith to Faith, From Glory to Glory

But the just shall live by faith [My righteous servant shall live by his conviction respecting man's relationship to God and divine things, and holy fervor born of faith and conjoined with it]; and if he draws back and shrinks in fear, My soul has no delight or pleasure in him.
Hebrews 10:38

If you and I want to move into new levels of glory, we must do so by moving into new levels of faith. Remembering that faith is confidence in God, we can say then that we need to move into new levels of confidence. We should be confident in every area of life.

God has dealt with me about being confident concerning my teaching gift. He always reminds me to be confident in the pulpit and to beware of insecure thoughts that sometimes try to get into my mind even while I am preaching. I am to go from the pulpit confidently into the next thing I need to do. I am to be confident in relationships, confident in prayer, confident when I am driving my car, confident when I make decisions, confident in every aspect of my daily life and ministry.

God has told me not to spend an hour in prayer and then go away thinking that I did not pray long enough or about the right things. He has shown me that I should do things confidently and remain confident after I have finished them.

I have often done things that I felt good about, until Satan started accusing me after I had finished. I finally realized that if I was doing the wrong thing, God would tell me ahead of time, not after I had finished and could do nothing about it.

We need to take a bold stand and declare, "I believe I hear from God. I believe I am led by His Spirit. I believe I make good decisions.

I believe I have a powerful prayer life. I believe people like me, and God gives me favor."

This kind of boldness does not mean we will never make mistakes. Making a mistake is not the end of the world as long as we are teachable. We dwell too much on the negatives and not enough on the positives.

I am sure that I make mistakes, that I don't hear from God perfectly. God told me long ago, "Joyce, don't worry about it; if you miss Me, I'll find you."

Instead of worrying about what we might do wrong, we should keep standing up on the inside and pressing forward, attempting to do something right. We can be so afraid of making a mistake that we end up never doing anything.

The Bible says the just shall live by faith, or confidence. We are going to interchange these words to make the message more practical. Sometimes faith seems so spiritual that we cannot see exactly how to apply it practically. It helps me to think of it in terms of confidence in God. So faith is confidence, and confidence is faith.

It does not pleasure God when you and I lose our confidence. Why? It saddens Him because of what we lose. It saddens God if we lose our confidence and let the devil steal from us the inheritance that He sent Jesus to die for us to have. God has done His part; now He wants us to do our part, which is to believe — to put our confidence in Him and His Word and live from faith to faith, so He can take us from glory to glory.

EXCEEDINGLY, ABUNDANTLY, ABOVE AND BEYOND ———

God:
...is able to [carry out His purpose and] do superabundantly, far over and above all that we [dare] ask or think [infinitely beyond our highest prayers, desires, thoughts, hopes, or dreams]. Ephesians 3:20

When I pray about or simply meditate on all the people who are hurting, I have a strong desire to help them all. I sometimes feel that my desire is bigger than my ability, and it is — but it is not bigger than God's ability!

When the thing we are facing in our life or ministry looms so big in our eyes that our mind goes "tilt," we need to *think in the spirit*. In the natural, many things are impossible. But in the supernatural, spiritual realm, with God nothing is impossible. God wants us to believe for great things, make big plans and expect Him to do things so great it leaves us with our mouths hanging open in awe. James 4:2 tells us we have not because we ask not! We can be bold in our asking.

Sometimes in my meetings people will approach the altar for prayer and sheepishly ask if they can request two things. I tell them they can ask God for all they want to, as long as they trust Him to do it His way, in His timing.

When you pray, do it standing up on the inside. What I mean is, do it respectfully, yet aggressively and boldly. Don't pray fearfully, and don't pray what I call "just" prayers.

As I listen to myself and others pray, it seems we frequently say, "Lord, if You will *just* do this or that...," "God, if You will *just* set me free in this area...," "Father, if You will *just* get me a raise or a promotion on my job...," "Master, we *just* ask You to help us in this area."

I know part of that is habit, but I believe it goes deeper than that. Most people say things like that in prayer, and I doubt that everyone would have the same habit. I believe it stems from an imbedded attitude within us that God really does not want to do much for a *dead dog or a grasshopper like us,* so we better not ask for much — only what we can barely get by with.

"Just do this or that" sounds like we are talking to someone who does things in a scanty way, someone who isn't able to do much. Our

prayer is, "If You will *just* do this one thing, we won't expect anything else." It makes us sound like people who really don't expect to get much, and if we can get *just* this one thing, we will be satisfied.

I recall God saying that He is *the Almighty God* (Genesis 17:1), in other words, "more than enough." The Bible says that Abram was *extremely* rich, not just barely getting by. (Genesis 13:2.) David was so wealthy, he had *provided for the house of the Lord 100,000 talents of gold, 1,000,000 talents of silver...* (1 Chronicles 22:14) and more.[2]

God regularly promoted plain, ordinary people into positions that they could never have gotten for themselves. The very word *prosperity* indicates more than what is needed. God wants us to prosper in every area, not just financially. He also wants us to have social, physical, mental and spiritual prosperity.

Think about it. God wants us to have so many invitations to minister that we have to choose which ones to accept. It is not God's will that His people be bored and lonely. He wants us to enjoy great fellowship and companionship. He wants us to feel great physically, not just drag our bodies around every day. He wants us to be vibrant and energetic, to enjoy life and live it to the fullest. He also wants us to be sharp mentally, have good memories and not live in a confused and worried manner.

You may be thinking, "Well, if that is God's will, why don't I have all those things in my life?"

Maybe you have not been asking for enough. Perhaps when you pray you don't do it boldly, standing up on the inside. Don't pray "just" prayers, pray for all you can *dare* to ask, think or desire.

When I pray for ministry opportunities so I can help more people, I go ahead and pray to be able to help every person on the face of the earth. I know it sounds really big, but in Ephesians 3:20 God is challenging us to pray for big things.

I always declare that our Life In The Word television program is seen every day, in every nation, city and town. Through satellite that vision is becoming more of a reality every day.

When our desires seem overwhelmingly big, and we don't see the way to accomplish them, we should remember that even though we don't know the way, we know the Waymaker! I will be dealing with the subject of confidence in prayer more completely in another chapter.

God has a way for us to do everything He places in our heart. He does not put dreams and visions in us to frustrate us. We must keep our confidence all the way through to the end, not just for a little bit and then when it looks like the mountain is too big, give up!

It is untold what people can do — people who don't *appear* to be able to do anything. God does not usually call people who are capable; if He did, He would not get the glory. He frequently chooses those who, in the natural, feel as if they are in completely over their heads but who are ready to stand up on the inside and take bold steps of faith as they get direction from God.

We usually want to wait until we "feel ready" before we step out, but if we feel ready then we tend to lean on ourselves instead of on God.

Know your weaknesses and know God — know His strength and faithfulness. Above all else, don't be a quitter.

Hebrews 10:38,39 in *THE MESSAGE* paraphrase Bible gives us very plain instructions on how God views quitters, the fearful and those who don't finish what they start:

> *You were sure of yourselves then. It's **still** a sure thing! But you need to stick it out, staying with God's plan so you'll be there for the promised completion.*
> *"It won't be long now, he's on the way; he'll show up most any minute.*

But anyone who is right with me thrives on loyal trust;
if he cuts and runs, I won't be very happy."
But we're not quitters who lose out. Oh, no! We'll stay with it
and survive, trusting all the way.

I have made up my mind not to be a quitter. In Colossians 3:2, the Apostle Paul tells us to set our minds and keep them set. Don't say things like, "This is just too hard," "I can't do this," or "I don't think I'll make it." Instead boldly proclaim, "I can do all things through Christ Who strengthens me. I am ready for anything, I am equal to anything, through the One Who infuses inner strength into me. I am self-sufficient in His sufficiency." (Philippians 4:13.)

FROM THE PIT TO THE PALACE

When Joseph had come to his brothers, they stripped him of his
[distinctive] long garment which he was wearing;
Then they took him and cast him into the [well-like] pit
which was empty; there was no water in it.
Genesis 37:23,24

And Pharaoh said to Joseph, Forasmuch as [your] God has
shown you all this, there is nobody as intelligent and discreet
and understanding and wise as you are.
You shall have charge over my house, and all my people shall
be governed according to your word [with reverence, submis-
sion, and obedience]. Only in matters of the throne will I be
greater than you are.
Genesis 41:39,40

A pit is a ditch, a trap, a snare. It refers to destruction. Satan always wants to bring us into the pit.

We know from Scripture that Joseph was sold into slavery by his brothers who hated him. They actually threw him into a pit and intended to leave him there to die, but God had other plans. They ended up selling him to slave traders, and he became the slave of a wealthy ruler in Egypt. Even though he was sold as a slave, he did not have a slave mentality. He believed he could do great things.

Everywhere Joseph went, God gave him favor. He even found favor in prison where he spent many years for an offense he did not commit. Ultimately, he ended up in the palace, second in command to Pharaoh, the ruler over all Egypt.

How did Joseph get from the pit to the palace? I believe it was by remaining positive, refusing to be bitter, being confident and trusting God. Even though it looked like he was defeated on many occasions, he kept standing up on the inside.

Joseph had a right attitude. Without a right attitude, a person can start in the palace and end up in the pit, which actually happens to a lot of people. Some, it seems, have great opportunities given to them, and they do nothing with their lives, while others who get a very bad start in life, overcome all obstacles and succeed.

Joseph was a dreamer; he made big plans. (Genesis 37:5-10.) The devil does not want us to have dreams and visions of better things. He wants us to sit around and be "do-nothings."

I challenge you to make your mind up right now to do something great for God. *No matter where you started, you can have a great finish.* If people have mistreated and abused you, don't waste your time trying to get revenge — leave them in God's hands and trust Him to bring justice in your life.

Know what you want out of life, what you want to do. Don't be vague! To be confident means to be bold, open, plain and straightforward — that does not sound like a vague, sheepish, fearful individual who is uncertain about everything. Decide to leave your mark in this world. When you depart from this earth, people should know that you have been here.

Every time I put hundreds of hours into a book project, I believe that people will be reading the book long after I am gone from the earth. I believe people will be watching my videos and listening to my tapes fifty, one hundred or even several hundred years from now, if the Lord should tarry. Believing that helps energize me to do the work that is involved in each project. I want to leave a legacy here in the earth when I go home to be with the Lord.

Now let's talk about a man in the Bible who lost his confidence. This is one of my favorite stories in God's Word.

"DON'T JUST LIE THERE, DO SOMETHING!"

Later on there was a Jewish festival (feast) for which Jesus went up to Jerusalem.

Now there is in Jerusalem a pool near the Sheep Gate. This pool in the Hebrew is called Bethesda, having five porches (alcoves, colonnades, doorways).

In these lay a great number of sick folk — some blind, some crippled, and some paralyzed (shriveled up) — waiting for the bubbling up of the water.

For an angel of the Lord went down at appointed seasons into the pool and moved and stirred up the water; whoever then first, after the stirring up of the water, stepped in was cured of whatever disease with which he was afflicted.

There was a certain man there who had suffered with a deep-seated and lingering disorder for thirty-eight years.

When Jesus noticed him lying there [helpless], knowing that he had already been a long time in that condition, He said to him, Do you want to become well? [Are you really in earnest about getting well?]

The invalid answered, Sir, I have nobody when the water is moving to put me into the pool; but while I am trying to come [into it] myself, somebody else steps down ahead of me.

Jesus said to him, Get up! Pick up your bed (sleeping pad) and walk!
Instantly the man became well and recovered his strength and picked up his bed and walked....
John 5:1-9

Why had this man been lying there thirty-eight years? It was because he was not only sick in his body, he was also sick in his soul. Sicknesses of the soul are much worse, and sometimes harder to deal with, than sicknesses of the body. I believe his condition (body and soul) had stolen his confidence. Having no confidence, he never really tried to do anything, at least not in an aggressive manner.

Notice that when Jesus asked him if he was in earnest about getting well, his answer was, "Sir, I have nobody to help me into the water. Somebody else always gets ahead of me." I have to believe that in thirty-eight years he could have scooted to the edge of the pool and been ready to fall in when the angel came and stirred up the water.

People who have lost their confidence usually become passive and even lazy. They don't believe they can do anything, so they want everyone else to do things for them.

Jesus did not stand and pity the man. Instead, He gave a very specific instruction. "Get up! Pick up your bed and walk!" In other words, *"Don't just lie there, do something!"*

Do you have a physical affliction that makes you feel insecure? Are you allowing circumstances to steal your initiative? Do you lack confidence because you are single or because you don't have a college education? Are you feeling sorry for yourself instead of standing up on the inside and being determined to overcome every obstacle?

Jesus knew self-pity would not deliver the man, so He didn't feel sorry for him. He had compassion on him, and that is different from

180

emotional pity. Jesus wasn't being harsh, hard or mean — He was trying to get the man set free!

Self-pity can be a major problem. I know, because I lived in self-pity for many years, and it was a problem for me, my family and the plan of God for my life. God finally told me that I could be pitiful or I could be powerful, but I could not be both. If I wanted to be powerful, I had to give up self-pity.

Like Joseph, I felt I had been thrown into a pit. Sexually abused for approximately fifteen years and growing up in a dysfunctional home had left me lacking confidence and filled with shame. I wanted to be in the palace (have good things in my life), but I seemed stuck in the pit (of emotional torment and despair).

"Why me, God?" was the cry of my heart, and it filled my thoughts and affected my attitude daily. This troubled mind and defeatist attitude caused me to have a chip on my shoulder and to expect everyone else to fix my problem. I felt like I was due something for the way I had been treated in life, but I was looking to people to pay me back when I should have been looking to God.

Like the man in John 5, Jesus did not give me pity either. He was actually very stern with me — but it was a turning point in my life. I am not in the pit any longer — I now have a great life. Like Lazarus coming out of the tomb, I shook off the graveclothes and began standing up on the inside.

"CAST OFF THE GRAVECLOTHES!"

> *And when he thus had spoken, he cried with a loud voice, Lazarus, come forth.*
> *And he that was dead came forth, bound hand and foot with graveclothes: and his face was bound about with a napkin. Jesus saith unto them, Loose him, and let him go.*
> *John 11:43,44 KJV*

When Jesus called Lazarus from the dead, He said, *Lazarus, come forth*. Then He said a second thing, "Take off his graveclothes."

Many people are born again, they have been raised to new life, yet they have never entered into that new life because they have the graveclothes of the past wrapped about them.

Be firm. Make a decision. Set your mind, stand up on the inside, and you also can go from the "pit to the palace."

Wilt Thou Be Made Whole?

> There was a certain man there who had suffered with a deep-seated and lingering disorder for thirty-eight years.
> When Jesus noticed him lying there [helpless], knowing that he had already been a long time in that condition, He said to him, Do you want to become well? [Are you really in earnest about getting well?]
> John 5:5,6

The *King James Version* of John 5:6 words Jesus' question to the man as, *...Wilt thou be made whole?*

If you and I want to get well (get over the past), we must do things God's way. I have great compassion for people reading this book — for you — and I say the same thing to you that the Lord said to me:

You can be pitiful or you can be powerful!

Stop comparing your circumstances with those of someone who is better off than you are. Find someone who is worse off than you are, and then you will feel better. Look at people who are in a better situation than you are only to get a vision of where you can be, not to compare yourself with them. Stand up on the inside and tell yourself, "God is no respecter of persons; if He did good things for these people, He will do the same for me."

Don't let your thoughts be down and negative, speak positively about your future. When you find it necessary to speak of the unpleasant past, always say, "God will work it out for my good."

SHAKE IT OFF!

Now Paul had gathered a bundle of sticks, and he was laying them on the fire when a viper crawled out because of the heat and fastened itself on his hand.

When the natives saw the little animal hanging from his hand, they said to one another, Doubtless this man is a murderer, for though he has been saved from the sea, Justice [the goddess of avenging] has not permitted that he should live.

Then [Paul simply] shook off the small creature into the fire and suffered no evil effects.

Acts 28:3-5

When Paul and his traveling companions were shipwrecked on the island of Malta, he was gathering sticks to make a fire and dry out when he was bitten by a snake that had been driven out of the flames. The Bible says that he simply shook it off into the fire. You and I should do the same — we too should be bold inwardly and shake it off!

Whatever may be troubling you from the past, *shake it off!* God has a great future planned for you. The dreams of the future have no room for the snake bites of the past!

I am trying to build a fire in you that will never go out. Stir yourself up and refuse to take on a spirit of coldness and deadness. Fight those negative thoughts that are holding you in bondage. Jesus wants to make you whole. He doesn't want to fix part of you, He wants to fix all of you: body, emotions, mouth, mind, attitude, will and spirit.

Jesus dealt with the man in John 5 in more than one area. He dealt with some issues in his soul before He healed his body. If we have sickness in our soul, it will continue showing up in our bodies in one way or another. We can receive healing in one area and have a problem pop up in another. We need to get to the root of our problems.

God wants to make you whole, completely whole. Don't be satisfied with anything less. Keep pressing on until every area of your life is healed.

God is on your side, and if He is for you it really does not matter who is against you. The giants may be big, but God is bigger. You may have weaknesses, but God has strength. You may have sin in your life, but God has grace. You may fail, but God remains faithful!

Wilt thou be made whole? If so, examine every attitude and any that do not line up with the Word of God — *eliminate!*

BE PERSISTENT IN FAITH!

> *...when the Son of Man comes, will He find [persistence in] faith on the earth?*
> *Luke 18:8*

We must deal sternly with our flesh — not allow it to rule. When Jesus comes back, He wants to find us in faith (confidence), not in self-pity or bitterness, fear or discouragement.

In this passage from Luke, Jesus asks, "When the Son of Man comes, will He find faith on the earth?" God is pleased with us as long as we keep believing. Our job is to maintain our confidence at a high level.

Will you make a decision to start living from faith to faith, from confidence to confidence? If you will, James 4:10 assures you that *...[He will lift you up and make your lives significant].*

Don't you just love that Scripture? Satan hates it, but I love it. Hallelujah, *He will lift you up and make your life significant!* Believe it, receive it and be confident that it will come to pass.

11

CONDEMNATION DESTROYS CONFIDENCE

11
CONDEMNATION DESTROYS CONFIDENCE

In order to be bold, one must be confident. We have established that confidence is vital to success. Everyone desires to be confident, and yet many people, perhaps even most people, have serious problems in this area. Why? There are many possible reasons: an abusive past, a poor self-image, ignorance of the love of God, rejection from family and peers, etc. But I believe one of the biggest reasons is condemnation.

And, beloved, if our consciences (our hearts) do not accuse us [if they do not make us feel guilty and condemn us], we have confidence (complete assurance and boldness) before God.
1 JOHN 3:21

We have spoken about the problem of condemnation in other parts of the book, but we need to devote an entire chapter to the subject because of the number of lives that are being wrecked by it.

WHAT IS CONDEMNATION?

> There is therefore now no condemnation to those who are in Christ Jesus, who do not walk according to the flesh, but according to the Spirit.
> Romans 8:1 *NKJV*

In *Strong's Exhaustive Concordance of the Bible* the Greek word translated *condemnation* in this verse means an "adverse sentence."[1]

Vine's Complete Expository Dictionary of Old and New Testament Words tells us the Greek noun *krima* translated *condemnation* "denotes (a) 'the sentence pronounced, a verdict, a condemnation, the decision resulting from an investigation.'"[2]

The word translated *condemn* in various New Testament Scriptures means to "note against, i.e., find fault with — blame;"[3] "judge against;"[4] "pronounce guilty;"[5] "punish, damn."[6]

In light of Romans 8:1, does this sound like the kind of activity we Christians ought to be engaged in — especially against ourselves?

EXCESSIVE SELF-EXAMINATION

Examine yourselves as to whether you are in the faith. Test yourselves. Do you not know yourselves, that Jesus Christ is in you?...
2 Corinthians 13:5 NKJV

The Bible tells us to examine ourselves, and I wholeheartedly agree that we need to do so. We should examine ourselves to see if we have sin, and if so we should sincerely repent, then move on to living without that sin in our lives.

There is a great difference between examination and condemnation. Examination helps us prove to ourselves that we are in Christ and He is in us, and that in Him we have been set free of sin. Condemnation keeps us mired in the very sin we feel condemned about. It does not deliver us — it traps us! It weakens us and saps all our spiritual strength. We give our energy to feeling condemned rather than living righteously.

There is such a thing as excessive self-examination, and I personally believe it opens the door for much of the unbalance we see today in this area among God's children.

To be overly introspective and continually examining our every move opens a door to Satan. In the past I experienced multiple problems in this area, and I know for a fact that you and I cannot succeed at being ourselves until the problem is dealt with thoroughly and completely.

I can remember finding something wrong with almost everything I did. Either Satan accused me, or I made his job easy and did it to myself. If I spent time with friends, after I left them I always found something wrong that I had said or done. Then I began the cycle of guilt, those feelings of condemnation which always follow investigation and bring adverse judgment. I call it a cycle because when we allow this kind of bondage into our lives, it repeats itself over and over again. We no sooner get over one incident than another one comes up.

If I prayed, I never felt that I had prayed right or long enough. If I read my Bible, I felt I should have read more, or perhaps a different section. If I read a book that God was using to help me at the time and did not read my Bible first, then I felt condemned because I "probably should have read my Bible first and not a book." If I went shopping, I felt condemned because I spent money or bought something that was not a desperate need. If I ate, I felt that I had eaten too much or the wrong things. If I enjoyed any type of entertainment, I felt that I should have been working.

Although some of these feelings were vague, they were none the less tormenting and debilitating. They were destroying my confidence, and I firmly believe Satan is using the same type of warfare to destroy many other people's confidence.

My husband never went through these types of things. He hardly ever felt guilty. He simply dealt with issues in his life through prayer, repentance and believing the Word of God. He did not feel guilty when he made mistakes, and I could not understand that at all. I don't mean that he wasn't repentant — he was repentant, but he did not feel condemned and guilty. He knew the difference between conviction and condemnation, and I did not.

He did not sit around and examine himself all day long. There were times when I told him, "Dave, you should not have talked to those people in that tone of voice. You may have hurt their feelings." His response would be, "Joyce, I was not trying to hurt their feelings — I was simply expressing myself. If they got hurt, it's their fault, not mine."

In such instances, he did not sense any conviction in his heart. As far as he knew, his heart was right, and he did not believe he should spend his life being responsible for everyone else's emotional reactions and personal hang-ups.

This does not mean that Dave doesn't care about people. He cares very much, but he is not going to let other people's hypersensitivity and insecurity control him. He will pray for them, but he will not be controlled by them.

That is true freedom!

I, on the other hand, lived with a false sense of responsibility. I not only felt overly responsible for everything I did or even may have done wrong, but I also felt responsible for how everyone else responded. In my ministry to others there were numerous times when I found myself dealing with insecure, emotionally wounded people. My bold, straightforward personality and their wounds didn't always mix well. I would just be myself, and they would get terribly hurt or offended. When I realized that something was wrong, I would feel condemned.

Perhaps they would be responding oddly to me, or I would hear later from someone else that I had hurt them, and then I would be back in my cycle again. I would feel and think: "I did not act right. They got hurt, and it's all my fault, I have to change. I try and try, but I always seem to make the same mistakes over and over." Then it would be time to feel condemned again. I always thought something must be wrong with me — it was always me!

My husband, who was and is secure, had a balanced perspective on these issues. He did not want to hurt people, yet at the same time he knew he could not be something he wasn't. He realized that the world is full of all kinds of people, and not all of them are going to respond favorably. He knew that if he made himself responsible for all of their reactions to him it would steal from him the life that Jesus died to provide.

This does not mean that we can treat people any way we feel like treating them and just "blow it off" saying, "If they have a problem, that's their fault." If God convicts us of wrong behavior, we should repent and let Him help us change our ways. But if there is no conviction from God, and we simply are receiving satanic condemnation through our own lack of confidence, then we must stand against those things or we will be in a spiritual prison all of our life.

After years of agony, I finally experienced freedom in these areas. Strongholds that have been imbedded in our lives for a long time don't always come out quickly. We have to keep seeking our freedom and refuse to quit until we see the breakthrough God promises in His Word.

We must learn to listen to our heart and not our head and feelings. Dave listened to his heart, and I listened to my head and feelings — that is why he was enjoying life, and I was not.

CONVICTION OR CONDEMNATION?

> *And when He comes, He will convict and convince the world and bring demonstration to it about sin and about righteousness (uprightness of heart and right standing with God) and about judgment.*
> *John 16:8*

Jesus told the disciples that when the Holy Spirit came, He would have an intimate, personal ministry to them.

One of the things the Holy Spirit is responsible for is guiding believers into all truth, and He is the agent in the process of sanctification in believers' lives. This is partially accomplished by His convicting powers.

In other words, every time we are getting off track or going in a wrong direction the Holy Spirit convicts us that our behavior or decision is wrong. This is accomplished by a "knowing" in our spirit that what we are doing is not right.

When you and I feel convicted, we should repent and change our direction. No more and no less is required or acceptable. If we know how to and are willing to cooperate with the Holy Spirit, we can move on to spiritual maturity and release all the planned blessings of God in our lives. If, however, we ignore this conviction and go our own way, we will find the way very hard and difficult. Our lives will be unblessed and therefore unfruitful.

Satan does not want us to receive conviction, nor does he even want us to understand it. He always has a counterfeit for all the good things that God offers — something somewhat like what God offers, but which, if received, will bring destruction instead of blessing.

I believe Satan's counterfeit for true godly conviction is condemnation. Condemnation always produces feelings of guilt. It makes us feel "down" in every way. We feel "under" something heavy, which is where Satan wants us.

God, on the other hand, sent Jesus to set us free, to give us righteousness, peace and joy. (Romans 14:17.) Our spirits should be light and carefree, not oppressed and heavy with burdens that we are unable to bear. We cannot bear our sins, Jesus came to bear them. He alone is able to do so, and we must receive His ministry.

I spent years not understanding the difference between conviction and condemnation. When I felt convicted for my wrong actions, instead of repenting and receiving God's mercy and grace, I immediately felt condemned and went into my cycle of guilt and remorse.

In John 8:31,32 (KJV) Jesus tells us, *...If ye continue in my word,...ye shall know the truth, and the truth shall make you free.* I am so thankful for the truth that was made known to me by the indwelling Holy Spirit because it has truly set me free.

If you have problems in this area, you may be thinking, "Joyce, I don't want to feel this way, but I don't know how to stop the cycle and begin enjoying freedom." It is the anointing on the Word of God that will set you free: *He sends forth His word and heals them and rescues them from the pit and destruction* (Psalm 107:20).

Here are some Scriptures to meditate on that will build your faith for those times when you are attacked by feelings of guilt and condemnation. Use them as a weapon against Satan by speaking them out of your mouth. Tell him the same thing Jesus did when He was being attacked: **"It is written!"** (See Luke 4:4,8; Matthew 4:7.)

> *But He was wounded for our transgressions, He was bruised for our guilt and iniquities; the chastisement [needful to obtain] peace and well-being for us was upon Him, and with the stripes [that wounded] Him we are healed and made whole.*
> *Isaiah 53:5*
>
> *He who believes in Him [who clings to, trusts in, relies on Him] is not judged [he who trusts in Him never comes up for judgment; for him there is no rejection, no condemnation — he incurs no damnation]; but he who does not believe (cleave to, rely on, trust in Him) is judged already....*
> *John 3:18*
>
> *Therefore, [there is] now no condemnation (no adjudging guilty of wrong) for those who are in Christ Jesus, **who live [and] walk not after the dictates of the flesh, but after the dictates of the Spirit.***
> *For the law of the Spirit of life [which is] in Christ Jesus [the law of our new being] has freed me from the law of sin and of death.*
> *Romans 8:1,2*

> *Who shall bring any charge against God's elect [when it is]*
> *God Who justifies [that is, Who puts us in right relation to*
> *Himself? Who shall come forward and accuse or impeach those*
> *whom God has chosen? Will God, Who acquits us?]*
> *Who is there to condemn [us]? Will Christ Jesus (the*
> *Messiah), Who died, or rather Who was raised from the dead,*
> *Who is at the right hand of God actually pleading as He*
> *intercedes for us?*
> *Romans 8:33,34*
>
> *...for the accuser of our brethren, he who keeps bringing*
> *before our God charges against them day and night, has been*
> *cast out!*
> *Revelation 12:10*

Stay in the Word. Spend time with God regularly. Refuse to give up, and stop the excessive self-examination. Let God convict you, don't do it yourself.

Truly meek people do not spend excessive time thinking about what they did right or what they did wrong; they simply stay "in Christ."

That is what you should do. Stop feeling guilty and condemned and start feeling bold and free!

HOLY BOLDNESS

> *Finally, my brethren, be strong in the Lord, and in the power*
> *of his might.*
> *Ephesians 6:10 KJV*

As believers we are to be bold in the Lord and the power of His might. Sometimes we let a "wimpy" spirit get on us. We get cowardly and afraid to step out and do what God is leading us to say and do. We must regularly be reminded that God's Word says that He *...hath* *not given us a spirit of fear; but of power, and of love, and of a sound mind* (2 Timothy 1:7 KJV).

I personally like the word *power*. I believe we all want to be powerful. God has some great plans for each of us.

God has great plans for you!

But now I am going to tell you a little secret — fear will never stop coming against us. We must learn to do what God tells us to do whether we feel fear or not. We must "do it afraid" if necessary, but that's what boldness does; it does it anyway!

I always thought that as long as I felt fear, I was a coward, but I have learned differently. When God told Joshua repeatedly to fear not, He was actually letting him know that fear was going to attack him, but that he was to walk in obedience to what God had spoken.

We are not cowards because we feel fear. We are cowards only if we let fear rule our decisions.

According to Vine, the Greek word *phobos*, translated *fear* in English, "first had the meaning of 'flight,' that which is caused by being scared; then, 'that which may cause flight.'"[7] God wants us to stand firm in His might and not run.

Stand still and do what God has said to do!

Fear is a spirit that can produce physical and emotional symptoms. When fear is attacking us, we may feel shaky and weak or find ourselves sweating. It may take everything we can muster just to speak or move. None of that means that we are cowards. The Word of God does not say "sweat not, shake not, tremble not" — it says "fear not"! The way to conquer fear is to press on through it and get on the other side of it — the side of freedom.

You and I usually want our deliverance by some miraculous means. We would like for some friend to pray for us so that we experience the disappearance of the problem, or we want to go through a prayer line and have some minister make our fear go away. That would be nice we think, but it normally does not happen that way. God does do miracles, and when He does, it is wonderful, but often we are required to "walk things out."

Don't think something is wrong with you if you always seem to have to "go through" things and never seem to get a miracle. God has different plans for each of us, and if He requires us to "walk it out" and "go through" it, then He has His reasons.

Going through things and not running from them is one of the major tools God uses to cause us to grow up and to prepare us to be used by Him to help other people. If we never go through anything, we never gain a personal victory over Satan. When we "hang in there" personally with God and press through difficult things, "walking them out" and learning from them, then we get a victory that nobody can take away from us.

We don't need to be constantly looking for somebody else who knows God to win our victories for us. We need to learn to be victorious for ourselves.

I certainly believe in praying for one another. I honestly don't know what I would do if people did not pray for me all the time. I believe prayer encourages and strengthens us so we can "go through" and not give up. I believe in ministering to one another, but there comes a point in all of our lives where we must stop running from difficult things and let God do the work in us that needs to be done.

We need to be bold!

If that means confronting fear, then we should press through the fear and learn what it means to be truly strong in the Lord and in the power of His might!

TRUE BOLDNESS IS MORE THAN A LOUD VOICE —————

He who is slow to anger is better than the mighty, he who
rules his [own] spirit than he who takes a city.
Proverbs 16:32

There is a difference between someone being loud and obnoxious and truly being bold in the Lord. I have been loud all my life, but I have not always been bold. I could talk big, but my actions were frequently fearful.

When a person has a strong personality everyone always assumes that individual is bold, but that is not always the case. I have discovered that many people with "strong personalities" are secretly very fearful people. They sometimes have an overly aggressive attitude that can be a coverup for fears they don't want to face or deal with.

What I call "holy boldness" is a beautiful thing. It steps out in quiet obedience and obeys God no matter what the personal cost. It gives glory to God and does not think highly of itself and lowly of others who are less aggressive.

Loudness or fleshly aggression always draws attention to itself. Often it does its own thing instead of obeying God, and is critical and judgmental of quieter people who are also precious to the Lord.

It is important to realize that we all have different God-given personalities. Just because people have a quieter or milder personality does not mean they cannot also be bold. Actually, it is sometimes those very types of people we must look to in order to find true boldness.

As I said, I was always loud, often obnoxious and yet secretly fearful. I still have a strong personality, but I have changed. I know when to press forward boldly and when to wait, when to speak firmly and when to keep quiet.

199

We never have any of God's principles working properly in our life if we don't have balance in them. We cannot present a rough, harsh attitude and call it boldness. True boldness is filled with love and mercy. It is strong when it needs to be, but is also considerate of others.

It is imperative for the plan of God that the Church manifest holy boldness, not secretly live in fear and condemnation then present some fake attitude to the world that is devoid of all power. I honestly believe that perhaps 80 percent of all people who call themselves Christians feel condemned most of the time. There are very few people who truly know who they are in Christ and walk in the security of that truth.

People experience all kinds of insecurities about themselves. They are double-minded in making decisions because they are not sure they hear from God. They doubt themselves to such a degree that they won't step out in obedience and do the things God is leading them to do.

Yet when it comes to shouting and making noise, they have a corner on the market, especially those who consider themselves to be really stirred up and on fire for God.

If we are to be truly bold, we need to learn to control our emotions and be humble enough to allow God to use us and bless us as He sees fit.

CAN YOU STAND TO BE BLESSED?

Blessed (happy, fortunate, prosperous, and enviable) is the man who walks and lives not in the counsel of the ungodly [following their advice, their plans and purposes], nor stands [submissive and inactive] in the path where sinners walk, nor sits down [to relax and rest] where the scornful [and the mockers] gather.
But his delight and desire are in the law of the Lord, and on His law (the precepts, the instructions, the teachings of God) he habitually meditates (ponders and studies) by day and by night.

*And he shall be like a tree firmly planted [and tended] by the
streams of water, ready to bring forth its fruit in its season;
its leaf also shall not fade or wither; and everything he does
shall prosper [and come to maturity].*
Psalm 1:1–3

A fellow believer recently told me of a very expensive automobile
that had been given to him. This man had been faithful for many
years in the ministry. He had worked very hard and made many sacrifices. A group of businessmen who knew and loved him wanted to
bless him with a certain automobile they knew he really admired, but
could never own without supernatural intervention. The car cost sixty
thousand dollars.

The man told us he was thinking about selling it. We asked him
if that would offend or hurt the people who gave it to him, and he
responded that they had told him when they gave him the car that he
was free to do with it as he pleased. I remember asking him why he
would want to sell it since it was his dream come true. I remember his
exact words to me. He said, "I know I am in ministry and that I
shouldn't feel the way I do, but to tell you the absolute truth, I don't
feel worthy to drive a car that expensive."

This is another manifestation of a lack of boldness which comes
from insecurity and not really knowing who we are in Christ. If we
cannot even be bold enough to receive and enjoy the blessings of God
without feeling guilty and condemned, then we are certainly lacking
in an area that is very important. To begin with, God wants to bless
His children, and in addition to that, He wants us to be a blessing.
How can we bless someone else if we are not blessed ourselves?

I believe it takes boldness to be blessed. First, we have to pray
some bold prayers, and second, we have to be able to receive and enjoy
the blessings when they come.

I remember the way I once was, before God taught me about righteousness through Jesus Christ. I felt so bad about myself that I could not imagine God wanting to give me radical blessings. I could barely believe He would provide for my daily needs, let alone give me far above and beyond those needs. I did not possess the boldness in prayer to ask for things that were not desperate needs.

As I heard more and more teaching about God's plan to prosper His children, I ventured out in prayer and began asking for some things that were desires of my heart, but not vital necessities. I can still remember feeling uncomfortable trying to talk to the Lord about things like really nice clothes or a new wedding ring. The ring I was wearing at the time cost seventeen dollars. Dave had purchased one for me that cost approximately a hundred dollars when we got married. Then a few years later, while we were playing golf, I asked him to carry it in his pocket for me. He must have pulled it out with some golf tees and lost it on the golf course. By that time we had three small children and no money for wedding rings. I bought one at a Christian bookstore. It had a cross on the top of it and was very pretty, but I sure wanted a really nice one.

By this time in my life I was getting really serious in my relationship with God, and I had just completed my first long fast. I had fasted the entire month of February, asking God to help me walk in love. Afterwards, a woman in the church I attended came up to me at a service and handed me a box with the message, "God told me to give you this." When I opened the box, it contained a beautiful wedding ring with twenty-three diamonds on it. Of course, I was very excited, but I began to notice that I was uncomfortable wearing it. I felt like people might think I was trying to be a big shot, or that they might not understand that it was a gift and not an extravagance on my part. I was afraid of their judgment.

Another time I recall a woman giving me a fur coat, and I felt the same way. It was something I had secretly desired, and I believed God was blessing me by giving it to me, but I hardly ever wore it at first because I felt that people might judge me or think things about me that were not true. I was young in the ministry, and I wanted people to trust me and relate to me. I did not want them to think I was becoming a person with a "big shot" attitude who was flaunting expensive things.

Dave finally got strong with me and said something along these lines, "Listen, Joyce, you work hard, you make a lot of sacrifices to minister to people, and if you cannot receive a blessing from God without being afraid of what people will think, then you will be in some kind of emotional prison all of your life." He further instructed me to wear the coat and enjoy it. What he said didn't immediately change the way I felt, but it did cause me to realize that I needed to change my way of thinking or Satan would use it to make sure I never had anything I wanted.

We do, of course, want to use wisdom in this area. For example, I don't think we necessarily need to wear our very best things when going to minister to the poor and needy or to people in a third-world country like India where poverty is so rampant. Doing so might offend them or make them feel even worse about their situation. It could cause them to feel inferior, which would not be helping them at all. Our purpose in going to minister to others must always be to lift them up and encourage them, not to make them feel inferior and discouraged.

We want to be sensitive to how others feel, but if taken out of balance, our sensitivity can open a door for people to control us. As we all know, no matter what we do, there will usually be somebody who does not approve. The bottom line is, we must each know our own heart and follow what we really believe Jesus would have us do in specific situations.

Some people are so fearful that even if God did radically bless them, they could not stand it. To walk in the blessings of God, we must be bold. We cannot fear the judgment and criticism of other people. Jealousy and envy are spirits that love to operate through family and friends to steal the joy of our prosperity and success. Remember, we war not against flesh and blood, but against principalities and powers. (Ephesians 6:12.)

Don't get angry at people, but don't bow down to the wrong spirits (attitudes) trying to control you either.

Prosperity is God's will for you. Psalm 1 promises prosperity to those who delight in His law (His precepts and instructions) and who meditate on them day and night. In other words, those who give God and His Word first place in their lives can expect to prosper.

The Bible is filled with Scriptures that promise blessing and prosperity to those who love God and obey Him. Therefore those who do that should expect to be blessed. They should not be so insecure they cannot receive blessings when they come.

God does not want us to walk with a haughty, I-am-better-than-you attitude. But He does want us to receive graciously and thankfully what He chooses to give us.

Somebody recently reminded me of Joseph's coat, a special gift from his loving father, Israel. (Genesis 37:3,4.) It was apparently very beautiful, because his brothers were all jealous of it. As a matter of fact, they hated Joseph because of it — but their hatred did not keep him from wearing it.

We must enjoy what God gives us and listen to Him, not all the people around us who should be happy for us, but who are not spiritually mature enough to do so.

BOLD ENOUGH TO BE LED BY THE SPIRIT─────────

The wicked flee when no man pursues them, but the [uncompromisingly] righteous are bold as a lion.
Proverbs 28:1

If we intend to succeed at being ourselves, we must reach a point where we can be led by the Holy Spirit. Only God, through His Spirit, will lead us to succeed and be all we can be. Other people usually won't, the devil certainly won't and we are not able to do it ourselves without God.

Being led by the Spirit does not mean that we never make mistakes. The Holy Spirit doesn't make mistakes, but we do. Following the Spirit's leading is a process which can only be learned by doing. We start by stepping out into things we believe God is putting on our hearts, and we learn by wisdom and experience how to hear more clearly and definitely.

I say that boldness is required to be led by the Spirit because 1) only boldness steps out, and 2) only boldness can survive making mistakes. When insecure people make mistakes, they often will never try again. Bold people make many mistakes, but their attitude is, "I'm going to keep trying until I learn to do this right."

Those who suffer from condemnation usually don't believe they can hear from God. Even if they think they may have heard from God and do step out, a minor failure is a major setback to them. Each time they make a mistake, they come under a new load of guilt and condemnation. They end up spending all their time in the cycle. They make a mistake, feel condemned, make another mistake, feel condemned, and on and on.

This book was written to encourage you to step out in faith and to be all that God has called you to be. But what if you read this book, step out and two weeks later discover you made a mistake? Are you going to be bold enough to pray, wise enough to learn from your mistakes, and determined enough to go on — or are you going to feel condemned and go back to wasting your life?

There is no point in learning to be led by the Holy Spirit if we don't understand that we will make some mistakes while on the journey.

You will make mistakes! Just don't make the mistake of thinking you will never make mistakes. This is an unrealistic expectation that will set you up for devastation.

I don't go around all the time expecting to make mistakes, but I have mentally dealt with the fact that I do make mistakes sometimes. I am prepared mentally and emotionally not to be defeated by mistakes and problems when they do come.

Be bold. Be determined that you are going to be all God wants you to be. Don't hide behind fears and insecurities any longer. If you have already made major blunders in your life and have been living under condemnation because of them, this is the time to *press on!* You are reading this book for a reason. As a matter of fact, you are the very person I was led to write this book for. Take it personally, just as though God were talking directly to you through it. Be determined to press on toward victory.

When we make mistakes, often it embarrasses us. We feel stupid, and we wonder what in the world people will think of us. Actually there are various types of emotional responses to failure. We should remember that is exactly what they are — "emotional responses" — and not be controlled by them.

We cannot always control our emotions, but we don't have to be controlled by them!

I don't believe anyone has failed until that individual has stopped trying.

Don't look at mistakes as failures, look at them as learning tools. We learn more from our mistakes than any other thing in life. I can read the Bible and see plainly that it tells me not to disobey God, and I may know mentally what it says, but I *really learn* not to disobey God after I have done it and experienced the consequences.

Some say, "Well, I would rather be safe than sorry." But to them I say, "You may end up safe, but you will also be sorry."

I want to encourage you that you can be all God ever planned for you, in Christ. Don't be half of it or three quarters of it, but be all that God designed you to be. Do all He wants you to do, and have all He wants you to have. You will never enjoy God's fullness without His boldness. Condemnation destroys boldness, so don't stay under condemnation.

Proverbs 28:1 says that the wicked flee when no one is even pursuing them. The wicked are running all the time. They run from everything. But the uncompromisingly righteous are as bold as a lion. And whether you feel like it or not, you are righteous!

TWO KINDS OF RIGHTEOUSNESS

> *For He... [God] ...made Him... [Jesus] ...who knew no sin to be sin for us, that we might become the righteousness of God in Him.*
> 2 Corinthians 5:21 NKJV

It is impossible to avoid a life of condemnation without truly understanding biblical righteousness. Remember that condemnation destroys confidence; therefore, we must press on and gain understanding in these areas so we can be assured of freedom.

There are two kinds of righteousness we need to discuss: self-righteousness and God's righteousness. Self-righteousness is earned through right actions, whereas God's righteousness is given by grace through faith in Jesus Christ.

Self-righteousness leaves no room for human error. We can only have it if we do everything perfectly. As soon as we make a mistake, we no longer have it and feel bad because we have lost it.

God's righteousness, however, is quite the opposite. It has been provided for those of us who, even though we would like to be perfect, have faced the fact that we cannot be perfect (except in heart). We have tried living with our faith in ourselves and found that it does not work. We have now placed our faith in Jesus and have believed that He became our righteousness. As we put on Christ, we put on righteousness like a robe and learn to wear it boldly in our earthly walk:

> *For as many [of you] as were baptized into Christ [into a spiritual union and communion with Christ, the Anointed One, the Messiah] have put on (clothed yourselves with) Christ.*
> *Galatians 3:27*

> *I will greatly rejoice in the Lord, my soul will exult in my God; for He has clothed me with the garments of salvation, He has covered me with the robe of righteousness....*
> *Isaiah 61:10*

You and I must face reality. We cannot even hope to spend the rest of our earthly lives without losing our temper. We cannot be perfectly patient in every situation. We cannot be perfectly obedient and always hear perfectly from God.

Jesus did not come for those who are well, but those who need a physician. (Matthew 9:11,12.) He came for "imperfect me" and "imperfect you." He came so we can succeed at being ourselves, even if it does mean making some mistakes while we are becoming ourselves.

We certainly improve as we continue our faith walk, but if we ever attain to self-righteousness, then we really won't need a Savior.

Personally, I would rather need Jesus. I have become extremely attached to Him and don't care to even think of trying to live without Him. I don't even strive for self-righteousness anymore. Of course, I try to do the best I can, but I have accepted my state as a human being. I am letting God be God, but I am also letting myself be human.

Sometimes we put too much on ourselves. We try to do the impossible and, as a result, spend our lives frustrated and condemned. If we are going to beat up on ourselves every time we make a mistake, we are going to get a beating every day. Living under condemnation is like getting a beating. At least that is the way I feel when I am under it.

Just think about that phrase, "I am under condemnation." That is something we say real often, and the very phrase itself tells us that we are *under* something. Jesus died so we could be lifted, not so we could go on living *under* things.

CONDEMNATION AND LEGALISM VERSUS FREEDOM AND LIFE

The thief comes only in order to steal and kill and destroy. I came that they may have and enjoy life, and have it in abundance (to the full, till it overflows).
John 10:10

Those who have a legalistic approach to life will always experience a lot of condemnation. Legalists see only one way to do things; it is usually a very narrow way with no room for mistakes and certainly no room for individual creativity.

For example, legalistic people may think there is only one way to pray. They may be assured that they must be in a certain posture, perhaps with eyes closed. They may falsify their voice to make it sound very religious and use lots of fancy words to impress God. For them, prayer must be a certain length. They may feel they have to pray thirty minutes or an hour or whatever their particular standard may be. Anytime they do not follow the rules, condemnation results.

Legalistic people are also usually very judgmental. Not only do they have rules for themselves, they also want and expect others to follow their rules.

I remember when I was very legalistic and had my own certain way to pray. My husband, of course, prayed differently than I did, and I felt he was doing it all wrong. I walked and prayed, while he sat and looked out the window and prayed. I remember thinking that he could not possibly be "in the Spirit" if he was looking out the window. I might have wanted to look out the window also, but that would not have been a "religious posture"; therefore, I would not allow myself that enjoyment. If I had sat by the window, looked out with my eyes open while talking to God, and tried to call it prayer, I would have felt condemned. I found that I resented Dave's freedom, which is another trait of legalistic people.

Legalism and joy don't go together. In John 10:10 Jesus said He came so we could have and enjoy our lives. Prior to that statement He said that the thief comes only to kill, steal and destroy. The thief He was talking about was actually a religious attitude that was common among the people of His day. These were people who sought after self-righteousness and knew nothing of the God-kind of righteousness. Jesus came to bring light into the darkness, hope to the hopeless, rest to the weary and joy to the world. But that could not happen unless people gave up their own righteousness and received His.

I heard one man say that there is one sure way to tell when you are beginning to experience freedom: there will always be someone around with a religious spirit to judge and criticize you for your freedom and to try to bring you under condemnation and make you feel guilty. Yes, legalism and condemnation do go together like hand and glove.

If we truly desire to be free from condemnation, we must give up legalistic attitudes and mindsets. The Bible teaches us to stay on the narrow path; it does not teach us to be narrow-minded. Our way is not the only way, and someone else's way is not the only way.

In Christ there is room for creativity and freedom. He may lead one person to pray while walking, another to pray while lying flat on the floor with face buried in a pillow, and yet another to kneel by the bed with folded hands, head tilted up to heaven and eyes closed. A truly spiritual person knows it is not posture that impresses God, but heart attitude.

One thing legalists have problems with is right standing with God through Christ and not as a result of works. They want to be righteous, but it is self-righteousness they seek. Legalism and pride go together, and pride always needs something to be proud about. Since pride needs something to be proud of, proud people feel they must always be "working" at something.

Of course, God wants us to work, but spiritual works are different from fleshly works. We do God's work in obedience to Him, but our own works are most often the result of a fleshly plan that is intended to gain us something in ourselves. It is not something God has directed. We have directed it and expect God to reward us for it. We must learn that God is not for sale. We cannot buy His favor, His blessings or His approval with our good works.

The Apostle Paul said true Christians pride themselves in Christ Jesus and put no confidence in the flesh. (Philippians 3:3.) This is the proper attitude we are to have. Whatever we do right is due to God's goodness, not ours. We have no room to boast, no room at all. We have no room to judge others after we have properly assessed ourselves. We can only receive the free gift of God's love and grace, love Him in return and let His love overflow to others through us.

Once our confidence is no longer in the flesh, but in Christ, we are ready to seriously press on toward being all we can be. It might be said that we are "marked for success."

Sad to say, many Christians never get to the place of freedom from self-righteousness and condemnation. They always remain on the low level of struggling for self-righteousness, trying, failing and feeling condemned. There is a higher place for God's children: the heights of freedom from condemnation. You and I can enjoy high levels of confidence that fuel us to succeed at being ourselves.

Always remember that religious people don't approve of freedom, prosperity, righteousness or confidence. They are into bondage, burdens, poverty, condemnation and guilt.

I lived that way most of my life, and I am not going to do it any longer. Jesus died to set you and me *free,* but we must take a *bold* stand and *receive* all that He died to give us. We must flatly refuse to live *under condemnation.* When we sin, we must be quick to repent, then *receive forgiveness* and *press on!*

I have been judged critically for teaching people to like themselves and to live free from condemnation. Legalistic people live in fear that this kind of liberated teaching will open a door to evil. They say, "Joyce, you are giving people a license to sin."

For a while I backed off because I thought they might be right. "After all, they know more than I do," was what my mind said. "They have all the education and degrees."

But God began to show me that those who really love Him are certainly not looking for an excuse to sin; they are doing everything they can to stay out of sin. Anyone who really wants to sin will find a way to do it no matter what we teach.

People don't experience freedom when we teach legalism. They do experience it when we teach righteousness and freedom from condemnation. Legalism never brings people closer to God. It gets them all tied up in rules and regulations and leaves them no time to fellowship with the Lord. They are afraid of Him most of the time and have no interest in coming nearer to Him because they have failed in some way and are now in the guilt cycle.

Condemnation destroys personal relationship with God. It steals the enjoyment of fellowship with Him. It destroys confidence, prayer, joy, peace and righteousness.

Condemnation steals, kills and destroys! But the righteousness that is found in Jesus Christ brings freedom, joy and life in all its abundance!

12

CONFIDENCE IN PRAYER

12
CONFIDENCE IN PRAYER

I chose prayer as the subject of this final chapter because it is so central to any success. If you and I are going to succeed at being ourselves and succeed in life, then we must know how to pray and be willing to give prayer a place of priority in our daily lives.

Every failure is in essence a prayer failure.

Truly I tell you, whoever says to this mountain, Be lifted up and thrown into the sea! and does not doubt at all in his heart but believes that what he says will take place, it will be done for him. For this reason I am telling you, whatever you ask for in prayer, believe (trust and be confident) that it is granted to you, and you will [get it].
MARK 11:23,24

If we don't pray, the best thing than can happen is nothing, so that things will stay the way they are, which is frightening enough in itself. We all need change, and the way to get it is through prayer.

It doesn't do any good to pray if we don't have confidence (faith) in prayer.

I believe a lot of people are dissatisfied with their prayer life, and much of their dissatisfaction is caused by a lack of confidence in themselves and in their prayers. Many Christians today have questions about their prayer life and feel frustrated about it. Even those who are actively praying regularly testify that they are frustrated because they feel something may be missing; they are not sure they are doing it right.

I can relate to this situation because I felt that way myself for a lot of years. I was committed to praying every morning, but at the end of my prayer time I always felt vaguely frustrated. I finally asked God what was wrong with me, and He responded in my heart by saying, "Joyce, you don't feel that your prayers are good enough." It was right back to the old condemnation thing all over again. I was not enjoying prayer because I had no confidence that my prayers were acceptable. What if they were "imperfect"?

God had to teach me some lessons about praying in faith, about understanding that the Holy Spirit was helping me in prayer and that Jesus was interceding along with me. (Romans 8:26; Hebrews 7:25.) If two of the Persons of the Godhead were helping me, surely my imperfect prayers were perfected by the time they arrived at the throne of God the Father. This knowledge took a lot of pressure off of me, but I still needed to develop confidence in simple, believing prayer.

SIMPLE, BELIEVING PRAYER

> *And when you pray, do not heap up phrases (multiply words, repeating the same ones over and over) as the Gentiles do, for they think they will be heard for their much speaking.*
> *Matthew 6:7*

We must develop confidence in simple, believing prayer. We need the confidence that even if we simply say, "God, help me," He hears and will answer. We can depend on God to be faithful to do what we have asked Him to do, as long as our request is in accordance with His will. We should know that He wants to help us because He is our Helper. (Hebrews 13:6.)

Too often we get caught up in our own works concerning prayer. Sometimes we try to pray so long, loud, and fancy that we lose sight of the fact that prayer is simply conversation with God. The length or loudness or eloquence of our prayer is not the issue, it is the sincerity of our heart and the confidence we have that God hears and will answer us that is important.

Sometimes we try to sound so devout and elegant that we get lost. We don't even know what we are trying to pray about. If we could ever get delivered from trying to impress God, we would be a lot better off.

Several years ago God caused me to realize that when I had occasion to pray out loud in front of other people, I really was not talking to Him at all. I was actually trying to impress those listening with my eloquent, spiritual-sounding prayer. Simple, believing prayer comes straight out of the heart of the one praying and goes straight to the heart of God.

How often should we pray? First Thessalonians 5:17 says, *Be unceasing in prayer [praying perseveringly]* or as the *King James Version* puts it, *Pray without ceasing.*

If we don't understand simple, believing prayer, that instruction can come down upon us like a very heavy burden. We may feel that we are doing well to pray thirty minutes a day, so how can we possibly pray without ever stopping? We need to have such confidence about our prayer life that prayer becomes just like breathing, an effortless thing that we do every moment we are alive. We don't work and struggle at breathing, unless we have a lung disorder, and neither should we work and struggle at praying. I don't believe we will struggle in this area if we really understand the power of simple, believing prayer.

We should remember that it is not the length or loudness or eloquence of the prayer that makes it powerful — prayer is made powerful by the sincerity of it and the faith behind it.

If we don't have confidence in our prayers we will not pray very much, let alone pray without ceasing. Obviously the terminology "without ceasing" does not mean that we must be offering some kind of formal prayer every moment twenty-four hours a day. It means that all throughout the day we should be in a prayerful attitude. As we encounter each situation or as things come to our mind that need attention, we should simply submit them to God in prayer.

We see then that prayer cannot depend on assuming a certain posture or attitude or being in a certain place.

WE ARE THE PLACE OF PRAYER ——————————

>...*My house will be called a house of prayer for all peoples.*
>*Isaiah 56:7*

Under the Old Covenant, the temple was the house of God, the place of prayer for His people. Under the New Covenant we are now God's house, a building still under construction, but none the less His house, His tabernacle, His dwelling place. Therefore, we should be called a house of prayer:

>*For we are fellow workmen (joint promoters, laborers together) with and for God; you are God's garden and vineyard and field under cultivation, [you are] God's building.*
>*1 Corinthians 3:9*

>*Do you not discern and understand that you [the whole church at Corinth] are God's temple (His sanctuary), and that God's Spirit has His permanent dwelling in you [to be at home in you, collectively as a church and also individually]?*
>*1 Corinthians 3:16*

Ephesians 6:18 lets us know that we can pray anywhere at anytime about anything, and that we should be watchful to do so: *Pray at all times (on every occasion, in every season) in the Spirit, with all [manner of] prayer and entreaty. To that end keep alert and watch with strong purpose and perseverance, interceding in behalf of all the saints (God's consecrated people).* If we believe and practice Ephesians 6:18, it can be life changing and certainly prayer changing.

It seems even when we do think about some prayer concern, we almost always follow that thought with another type of wrong thinking: "I need to remember to pray about this during my prayer time."

Why don't we stop and pray right then? Because we have a mental stronghold in this area. We think we must be in a certain place, in a certain frame of mind and in a certain position before we can pray. It's no wonder we don't get much praying done. If the only time we can pray is when we are sitting still and doing absolutely nothing else, most of us certainly won't be praying without ceasing.

We should all set aside a time to spend with God when we are doing nothing else, and we should discipline ourselves to keep our appointments with Him. We are diligent to keep doctor, dentist and lawyer appointments, but somehow when it comes to God we feel we can change our appointments without notice or even not show up at all.

If I were God, I would be insulted!

Yes, we should have these set-apart times, but in addition to that we should be exercising our privileges of prayer all day long. Our prayers can be verbal or silent, long or short, public or private — the important thing is that we pray!

SECRET PRAYER

> *Also when you pray, you must not be like the hypocrites, for*
> *they love to pray standing in the synagogues and on the corners*
> *of the streets, that they may be seen by people. Truly I tell you,*
> *they have their reward in full already.*
> *But when you pray, go into your [most] private room, and,*
> *closing the door, pray to your Father, Who is in secret; and*
> *your Father, Who sees in secret, will reward you in the open.*
> *Matthew 6:5,6*

Although some prayers are public prayers or group prayers, most of our prayer life is secret and should be that way. In other words, we don't have to broadcast how much we pray and everything we pray about.

"Secret prayer" means a number of things. It means that we do not broadcast to everyone we know our personal experiences in prayer. We pray about the things and people God places on our heart, and we keep our prayers between us and Him unless we have a really good reason to do otherwise.

There is nothing wrong with saying to a friend, "I have been praying for the youth of our nation a lot lately," or, "I have been praying for people to enter into a more serious relationship with God." Sharing of this type is simply part of friendship, but there are things God places on our heart to pray about that we should keep to ourselves.

"Secret prayer" means that we do not make a display of our prayers to impress people. We see an example of the right and wrong way to pray in Luke 18.

HUMBLE PRAYER

> *Two men went up into the temple [enclosure] to pray, the one a Pharisee and the other a tax collector.*
> *The Pharisee took his stand ostentatiously and began to pray thus before and with himself: God, I thank You that I am not like the rest of men — extortioners (robbers), swindlers [unrighteous in heart and life], adulterers — or even like this tax collector here.*
> *I fast twice a week; I give tithes of all that I gain.*
> *But the tax collector, [merely] standing at a distance, would not even lift up his eyes to heaven, but kept striking his breast, saying, O God, be favorable (be gracious, be merciful) to me, the especially wicked sinner that I am!*
> *I tell you, this man went down to his home justified (forgiven and made upright and in right standing with God), rather than the other man; for everyone who exalts himself will be humbled, but he who humbles himself will be exalted.*
> *Luke 18:10-14*

For prayer to be properly called "secret prayer," it must come from a humble heart.

In this lesson on prayer taught by Jesus Himself, we see that the Pharisee prayed "ostentatiously," meaning that he prayed pretentiously, making an extravagant outward show. There was nothing secret or even sincere about his prayer. *The Amplified Bible* translation quoted above even says that he prayed "before and with himself." In other words, his prayers never got two inches away from himself; he was all caught up in what *he* was doing.

The second man in the story, a despised tax collector and a "wicked sinner" in most people's eyes, humbled himself, bowed his head and quietly, with humility, asked God to help him. In response to his sincere, humble prayer, a lifetime of sin was wiped away in a moment. This is the power of simple, believing prayer.

My ministry team and I have the privilege of leading thousands of people to the Lord each year in our conferences. Watching the people who respond to the altar call is phenomenal. I talk to them a few minutes and lead them in a very simple prayer of faith and surrender. In those few moments, a lifetime of sin is removed and righteousness takes its place through simple faith in Jesus Christ.

God has not given us a bunch of complicated, hard-to-follow guidelines. Christianity can be simple, unless complicated people make it complicated.

Build your faith on the fact that simple, believing prayer is powerful. Believe that you can pray anywhere, anytime, about anything. Believe that your prayers don't have to be perfect, or eloquent, or long. Keep them short and simple, full of faith — and fervent.

FERVENT PRAYER

....The effective, fervent prayer of a righteous man avails much.
James 5:16 NKJV

223

For prayer to be effective it must be fervent. However, if we misunderstand the word *fervent*, we may feel that we have to "work up" some strong emotion before we pray; otherwise, our prayers will not be effective.

I know there were many years when I believed this way, and perhaps you are likewise confused or deceived. Here are some other translations of this verse that may make its meaning more clear:

> ...*The earnest (heartfelt, continued) prayer of a righteous man makes tremendous power available [dynamic in its working].*
> *James 5:16 AMP*

> ...*The heartfelt supplication of a righteous man exerts a mighty influence.*
> *James 5:16 WEYMOUTH*

> ...*the prayers of the righteous have a powerful effect.*
> *James 5:16 MOFFATT*

> ...*Tremendous power is made available through a good man's earnest prayer.*
> *James 5:16 PHILLIPS*

I believe this Scripture means that our prayers must be truly sincere, coming out of our heart and not just our head.

At times I experience a great deal of emotion while at prayer, sometimes I even cry. But there are plenty of times when I don't feel emotional and don't cry; I am sincere in my praying, but I don't *feel* anything out of the ordinary.

Believing prayer is not possible if we base the value of our prayers on feelings.

I remember enjoying so much those prayer times when I could *feel* God's presence, and then wondering what was wrong during the times when I didn't *feel* anything. I learned after a while that faith is not based on *feelings* in the emotions, but on knowledge in the heart.

THE PRAYERS OF A RIGHTEOUS MAN

> *...The effective, fervent prayer of a **righteous** man avails much.*
> *James 5:16 NKJV*

James 5:16 states that the fervent prayer of a "righteous" man is powerful. This means a man who is not under condemnation — one who has confidence in God and in the power of prayer. It does not mean a man without any imperfection in his life.

The very next verse uses Elijah as an example: *Elijah was a human being with a nature such as we have [with feelings, affections, and a constitution like ours]; and he prayed earnestly for it not to rain, and no rain fell on the earth for three years and six months.*

Elijah was a powerful man of God who did not always behave perfectly, but he still prayed powerful prayers. He did not allow his imperfections to steal his confidence in God.

Elijah had faith, but he also had fear. He was obedient, but at times he was also disobedient. He was repentant, he loved God and wanted to know His will and fulfill His call upon his life. But sometimes he gave in to human weaknesses and tried to avoid the consequences of that will and calling.

In many ways Elijah was a lot like you and me. In 1 Kings 18 we see him moving in tremendous power, calling down fire from heaven and slaying 450 prophets of Baal at God's command. Then immediately afterwards, in 1 Kings 19 we see him fearfully running from Jezebel, becoming negative and depressed, and even wanting to die.

Like many of us, Elijah let his emotions get the upper hand. The fact that James 5:16 instructs us to pray powerful effective prayers like the righteous men and women of God — and then gives a discourse on Elijah and how he was a human being just like us, and yet prayed powerful prayers — should give us enough "scriptural power" to defeat condemnation when it rises up to tell us we cannot pray powerfully because of our weaknesses and faults.

MEN WHO PRAYED

> *Then he spoke a parable to them, that men always ought to pray and not lose heart.*
> *Luke 18:1 NKJV*

The Bible is filled with accounts of men and women who walked with God and who viewed prayer as the main business of their lives.

Jesus prayed:

> *And in the morning, long before daylight, He got up and went out to a deserted place, and there He prayed.*
> *Mark 1:35*

Surely prayer was important to Jesus; otherwise, He would have stayed in bed. Most of us don't get up early for anything unless it is very important.

We see that Jesus didn't make a big display of prayer. In this example He went to a private place, where the Bible simply says, "He prayed."

David prayed:

> *O God, You are my God, earnestly will I seek You; my inner self thirsts for You, my flesh longs and is faint for You, in a dry and weary land where no water is.*
> *Psalm 63:1*

David prayed what I call "seeking God" prayers. Many times a day I find myself whispering in my heart or even out loud, "Oh, God, I need You." This is simple, but powerful prayer. God responds to this kind of prayer. He helps us, manifests His Presence to us and is blessed by our dependence upon Him.

Other times I hear myself say to the Lord, "Father, help me with this." It has become a habit, one I hope I never manage to break.

The Bible says that we have not because we ask not. (James 4:2 KJV.) Why not ask for help frequently?

Daniel prayed:

> *Now when Daniel knew that the writing was signed, he went into his house, and his windows being open in his chamber toward Jerusalem, he got down upon his knees three times a day and prayed and gave thanks before his God, as he had done previously.*
> *Daniel 6:10*

Daniel certainly believed prayer was important. A royal decree had been issued that for thirty days anyone asking a petition of any god or man other than the king would be cast into a den of lions.

Daniel prayed the same as always. He apparently knew that God's protection was more important than man's threats.

The Apostles prayed:

> *But we will continue to devote ourselves steadfastly to prayer and the ministry of the Word.*
> *Acts 6:4*

The Apostles had become so busy with food distribution and other such mundane details that their administrative responsibilities were interrupting their prayer and study time. They selected seven men to help with these practical duties so they could continue to *devote* themselves to prayer and the Word of God.

Sometimes we have to change things in our lives to make plenty of room for prayer. We have to eliminate other things that are less fruitful. You and I will not succeed at anything unless we pray.

"I'm too busy" is the biggest and yet the lamest excuse we offer. We set our schedules (our priorities), and if we have any time left over after we have done everything else, then we pray. What we do with our time tells us what is important to us. If we don't pray, one of the reasons is because we don't see the value in it that we should.

History gives us records of many others since the Bible was written who have recognized both the value and the necessity of prayer.

Martin Luther reportedly said, "I have so much business I cannot get it done without spending three hours a day in prayer."

We might wonder how we could possibly devote three hours a day to prayer with all the other things we have to do, but Martin Luther realized that his attitude needed to be the exact opposite.

I am not suggesting that everyone must pray three hours a day. The point is that even very busy people with very important things to do have made ample time for prayer.

John Wesley reportedly said, "God does nothing except in answer to prayer."

In the Christian life, prayer is not optional. If we want to get anything accomplished in life, we must pray.

Moses prayed and changed God's mind.

PRAYER CHANGES THINGS AND PEOPLE

> *And the Lord said to Moses, I have seen this people, and
> behold, it is a stiff-necked people;*

*Now therefore let Me alone, that My wrath may burn hot
against them and that I may destroy them; but I will make of
you a great nation.*

*But Moses besought the Lord his God, and said, Lord, why
does Your wrath blaze hot against Your people, whom You
have brought forth out of the land of Egypt with great power
and a mighty hand?*

*Why should the Egyptians say, For evil He brought them
forth, to slay them in the mountains and consume them from
the face of the earth? Turn from Your fierce wrath, and
change Your mind concerning this evil against Your people.*

*[Earnestly] remember Abraham, Isaac, and Israel, Your
servants, to whom You swore by Your own self and said to
them, I will multiply your seed as the stars of the heavens,
and all this land that I have spoken of will I give to your
seed, and they shall inherit it forever.*

*Then the Lord turned from the evil which He had thought to
do to His people.*

Exodus 32:9-14

There are several other examples similar to this one in the Bible,
situations that depict how sincere prayer can change God's mind.

There are times when I can sense that God is getting weary of
putting up with someone who is not obeying Him, and I will find
myself being led to pray for God to be merciful to that person and to
give that individual another chance. I am sure others prayed that for
me at times when I needed it.

As Jesus told His disciples at Gethsemane, we should "watch and
pray." (Matthew 26:41 KJV.) We need to pray for one another, not
judge and criticize each other. There is a time when we don't need to
pray anymore for people or situations; we need to leave them in God's
hands. There are times when people will be better off in the long run

if God does deal severely with them now. We need to be Spirit-led in our praying, but we must pray.

If we watch people, we can see when they need encouragement, when they are depressed, fearful, insecure or experiencing any number of other obvious problems. God's allowing us to discern their need is our opportunity to be part of the answer. We can pray and take whatever action the Lord may lead us to take. We should set ourselves to be part of the answer to people's problems, not part of the problem. Talking to others about what is wrong with people we know does not meet their need. Instead, we should pray!

I recently saw two women coming out of a doughnut shop, and both of them were about 100 to 150 pounds overweight. They were each carrying an entire box of doughnuts, and I could sense they had a serious problem with their emotions and were eating to comfort themselves. I simply prayed, "God, help those two women lose weight, and help them know that You are the answer to their problem. Send the perfect laborer into their lives, someone who can speak a word in season to them, amen."

I don't think people are ever offended because we pray for them. There have been times in my life when I needed to lose weight, and I hoped someone was praying for me. I would much rather have people's prayers than their judgment.

Too often we see situations like this and think, "What a shame — the last thing they need is a doughnut," or we go tell someone else what we have seen, but we fail to do the one thing that can make a difference. We can pray!

However, we won't pray about these kinds of situations if we have a wrong attitude concerning prayer. If we think we must be in a certain place, in a certain posture, in a certain "spiritual" frame of mind, Satan will rob us of our prayer, and much of God's work will not get done.

Sometimes as Christians we over-spiritualize things to the point that we cannot do them, let alone enjoy them. I believe if people understood the simplicity of prayer they would pray more because they would be able to enjoy it and not feel they were always *working* at it.

For years I tried to change my husband, my children and myself, until God finally convicted me that I was working, not praying. He showed me that I needed to do the praying and let Him do the working.

I suggest you do the same thing.

Who do you have on your potter's wheel? If you think of anyone, do yourself and them a favor and let them off.

We are not the potter, God is, and we certainly don't know how to "fix" people. We can sometimes see what we feel is a problem in a person's life, but we don't know how to fix it because we don't know what broke it in the first place.

Let us take the two ladies at the doughnut shop as an example. I could see the problem — they were extremely overweight. But I did not know *why* they were overweight. Perhaps they were undisciplined, but I did not sense that was the case. Perhaps they had both been physically, mentally or sexually abused. Perhaps they had endured a lifetime of rejection and emotional pain. They may have been filled with shame and actually started eating as a personal comfort and then fell into a trap from which they could not escape.

When we try to *fix* people, we often hurt them worse because we *assume* a lot of things that may or may not be true about them. People who are hurting don't need someone with a spirit of pride trying to fix them, they need acceptance, love and prayer.

In my own pride I tried to fix my family, and the result was I actually drove them away. Finally, I realized I wasn't getting what I wanted because I was not praying and trusting God to fix them in His own timing and way. The amazing thing is that now either God fixed them or He fixed me, because I like them the way they are. Either way, without my even knowing when or how, He took care of the problem.

Pray! Pray! Pray! It is the only way to get things accomplished in God's economy. God has His guidelines and "you have not because you ask not" (James 4:2 KJV, author's paraphrase) is one of them. If we do things His way, we always get good results. If we do things our way, we always end up miserable with no results.

POWER AND AUTHORITY THROUGH PRAYER

> *And I tell you, you are Peter [Greek,* **Petros** *— a large piece of rock], and on this rock [Greek,* **petra** *— a huge rock like Gibraltar] I will build My church, and the gates of Hades (the powers of the infernal region) shall not overpower it [or be strong to its detriment or hold out against it].*
> *I will give you the keys of the kingdom of heaven; and whatever you bind (declare to be improper and unlawful) on earth must be what is already bound in heaven; and whatever you loose (declare lawful) on earth must be what is already loosed in heaven.*
> *Matthew 16:18,19*

Since we are not only physical creatures but spiritual beings as well, we are able to stand in the physical realm and affect the spiritual realm. This is a very definite privilege and advantage.

For example, if I have a grandchild who is experiencing difficulties in school, I can go into the spiritual realm through prayer and bring about action that will cause change in that situation. *God is a Spirit...* (John 4:24), and every answer we need to every situation is with Him.

When I say we can "go into the spiritual realm," I am not trying to sound spooky or even overly spiritual. Each of us who prays sincerely goes into the spiritual realm through our prayers. We are here on earth in body, but in spirit we go to the place where God is and there make a request of Him in faith.

In Matthew 16:19, Jesus told Peter that He would give him the keys of the kingdom of heaven. Keys unlock doors, and I believe those keys (at least in part) can represent various types of prayer. In His conversation with Peter, Jesus went on to teach him about the power of binding and loosing, which operates on the same spiritual principle.

Jesus was also speaking to Peter about the power of faith in verse 18, and we know that one way faith is released is through prayer. The power of binding and loosing is also exercised in prayer.

In Jesus' name we can bind (hinder) the devil, and in His name we can loose angels by requesting that they be dispatched from heaven to provide protection for ourselves or for others. (Matthew 26:53; Hebrews 1:7,14.)

When you and I pray about deliverance from some bondage in our lives or in the life of another, we are in effect, binding that problem and loosing an answer. The act of prayer binds evil and looses good.

In Matthew 18 we see Jesus dealing again with this issue of binding and loosing, only this time He is adding instructions about praying in agreement and emphasizing how much power that type of prayer carries.

Praying Down God's Will

Truly I tell you, whatever you forbid and declare to be improper and unlawful on earth must be what is already forbidden in heaven, and whatever you permit and declare proper and lawful on earth must be what is already permitted in heaven.

Again I tell you, if two of you on earth agree (harmonize together, make a symphony together) about whatever [anything and everything] they may ask, it will come to pass and be done for them by My Father in heaven.
Matthew 18:18,19

I would call your attention to the fact *The Amplified Bible* makes it clear that our authority is to bring what God wills to earth, not to bring our own will to pass. Prayers that are outside of the will of God will not be answered except with a no!

As believers, we have spiritual authority and should exercise it. One of the ways we do that is in prayer. God desires to use His surrendered servants to pray His will down from heaven to earth, as we are taught by Jesus to pray: ...*Thy will be done in earth, as it is in heaven* (Matthew 6:10 KJV).

What an awesome privilege. Not only can our prayers affect our own destiny, but we ourselves can be used by God to help others succeed at being themselves and thereby experience the fullness of all He has planned for them in life.

SEVEN TYPES OF PRAYER TO PRAY WITH EASE

Pray at all times (on every occasion, in every season) in the Spirit, with all [manner of] prayer and entreaty....
Ephesians 6:18

Now I would like to discuss the seven types of prayer we see in the Word of God. We should be exercising on a regular basis all the various types of prayer. They are simple, can be prayed anywhere at anytime and are most effective when prayed from a believing heart.

THE PRAYER OF AGREEMENT

First, let me say that I believe this prayer can only be prayed by two or more people who are committed to living in agreement. This prayer is not for people who generally live in strife and then decide they need to agree for some type of miracle because they are desperate. God honors the prayers of those who pay the price to live in unity.

Because our prayer power multiplies when we are in agreement with those around us (1 Peter 3:7), we need to be in agreement all the time, not just when we face a crisis situation. There will be times in our life when what we are up against is something that is bigger than we are by ourselves. At such times, we will be wise to pray together with someone who is in agreement with us in that situation. Let me give you an example.

Dave and I often pray in agreement while driving down the highway. We are trying to break ourselves of the bad habit of "talking about praying later" and to develop a new habit of "praying right away." When possible, we hold hands as we pray in agreement. I don't think there is anything "magic" about holding hands in prayer — but in our case touching each other seems to indicate that we are indeed in agreement, not only about a certain issue, but in general.

If you feel you have nobody in your life with whom you can agree in prayer, don't despair. You and the Holy Spirit can agree. He is here on the earth, with you and in you as a child of God.

Many people will never succeed at being themselves simply because they cannot even get into agreement with God.

I recall a woman who now works for me once saying that she could not believe it when God initially began placing it in her heart that she was going to work on my staff full time. This woman had been a housewife for thirty-five years and was having a difficult time believing that she could do anything else. Her children were grown, and it was time for her to enter a new season in life. God kept encouraging her to apply for a position in our ministry, and she kept telling Him she was not able, that she did not know how to do any of the things we needed done.

Not only was the Lord encouraging her to apply for a position with us, but He was simultaneously placing it in her heart to go to Bible college at her home church for a year before coming to work for us. She was absolutely certain in her "flesh" that she could do neither of these, but she finally fell to her knees and said: "Holy Spirit, I agree with You. If You say I can do this thing, then I will believe I can do it." She did go to Bible college, and she did apply for a position with us. Now she has worked on our staff for approximately fourteen years.

There is power in agreement! Pray the prayer of agreement, especially when you feel the need for a little extra prayer power!

THE PRAYER OF PETITION

This prayer is by far the most often used, but perhaps it should not be, as you may agree later. When we petition God, we ask for something for ourselves. When we pray for others, we are interceding (we will discuss that type of prayer later). Most of us, sorry to say, are overly interested in ourselves. For that reason, we frequently exercise our right to petition God. It is, of course, not wrong to ask God to do things for us, but our petitions should be well balanced with praise and thanksgiving (also to be discussed later).

It is important to petition God about our future — to pray and ask Him for His help in allowing us to succeed at being ourselves. Our success won't come through personal struggle or vain effort. It will only come as a result of God's grace.

You and I must add our effort to His grace, but effort without grace is useless. Grace comes as a result of asking for it. Asking is praying the prayer of petition. Once again this type of prayer can be prayed with ease.

Each day as I sit down to write and work on my sermons or books, I ask God to help me. I do it briefly with no special posture or eloquent words, but I know I am calling forth the power of God to help me be all I can be that particular day.

You and I can be bold in petitioning God for any type of need in our lives. We are not restricted to a certain number of requests per day. We can feel at ease talking to God about anything that concerns us, and petitioning for our own needs and desires is one of the types of prayer we are told to pray.

THE PRAYER OF PRAISE AND THE PRAYER OF THANKSGIVING

Praise is a narration or a tale in which we recount the good things about an individual, in this case, God. We should praise the Lord continually. By continually, I mean all throughout the day. We should praise Him for His mighty works, the things He has created and even the things He is yet to do in each of our lives.

We should also thank Him always, in good times and especially in difficult ones. When prayers of petition outweigh prayers of praise and thanksgiving in our prayer life, I believe it says something about our character.

Greedy people ask, ask, ask and rarely ever appreciate what they have already received. I do not believe that God will release us into the fullness of all that He has planned for us until we become thankful for what we have already been given.

Consider these Scriptures and walk in obedience to them:

> *Speak out to one another in psalms and hymns and spiritual songs, offering praise with voices [and instruments] and making melody with all your heart to the Lord,*
> *At all times and for everything giving thanks in the name of our Lord Jesus Christ to God the Father.*
> *Ephesians 5:19,20*

*We continually give thanks to God the Father of our Lord Jesus
Christ (the Messiah), as we are praying for you.*
Colossians 1:3

*And whatever you do [no matter what it is] in word or deed,
do everything in the name of the Lord Jesus and in [depen-
dence upon] His Person, giving praise to God the Father
through Him.*
Colossians 3:17

*Be unceasing in prayer [praying perseveringly];
Thank [God] in everything [no matter what the circumstances may be, be thankful and give thanks], for this is the
will of God for you [who are] in Christ Jesus [the Revealer
and Mediator of that will].*
1 Thessalonians 5:17,18

*First of all, then, I admonish and urge that petitions, prayers,
intercessions, and thanksgivings be offered on behalf of all men.*
1 Timothy 2:1

*Through Him, therefore, let us constantly and at all times
offer up to God a sacrifice of praise, which is the fruit of lips
that thankfully acknowledge and confess and glorify His
name.*
Hebrews 13:15

Powerful living comes through thanksgiving. One of the ways we
can "pray without ceasing" is by being thankful all day long, praising
God for His goodness, mercy, loving-kindness, grace, long-suffering
and patient nature.

THE PRAYER OF INTERCESSION

To intercede means to *stand in the gap* for someone else. (Ezekiel
22:30.)

If there is a breach in people's relationship with God due to a particular sin in their life, we have the privilege of placing ourselves in that breach and praying for them. If they have a need, we can intercede for them and expect to see them comforted and encouraged while they wait. We can also expect a timely breakthrough for them concerning their need being met.

I don't know what I would do if people did not intercede for me. Literally thousands of people have told me over the years that they pray for me. I actually ask God for intercessors. I petition Him to give me people to intercede for me and for the fulfillment of the ministry to which He has called me.

We need each other! If our prayers are only filled with petition and are void of intercession, that also makes a statement about our character — just as when petition outweighs praise and thanksgiving in our prayer life.

I have discovered that the more I am delivered from selfishness, the more I pray for others — and vice versa.

Praying for others is equivalent to sowing seed. We all know that we must sow seed if we are to reap a harvest. (Galatians 6:7.) Sowing seed into the lives of other people is one sure way to reap a harvest in our own life. Each time we pray for someone else, we are assuring our own success.

If you want to succeed at being yourself, I highly recommend that you include ample intercession for others in your prayer life. Give away what you need or want.

If you want to be a success, help someone else succeed by praying for them. If you want your ministry to succeed, pray for someone else's ministry. If you want your business to succeed, pray for someone else's business. If you need a breakthrough over some bad habit that is hindering you and holding you back, pray for someone else who has a need in a similar area.

Remember, we are often tempted to judge, which only holds us in bondage. Give people prayer instead of judgment, and you will make much faster progress toward the fulfillment of your destiny.

THE PRAYER OF COMMITMENT

When we are tempted to worry or take the care of some situation in life, we should pray the prayer of commitment.

For example, if I have done my best to get to an appointment on time, and due to circumstances beyond my control it appears I am going to be late, instead of becoming frantic I have learned to pray the prayer of commitment. I say, "Lord, I am giving this situation to You; do something to make things work out right." I find that when I do that, things do work out all right. Either the Lord gives me favor with those I am supposed to meet and they totally understand, or I arrive and find they were also running behind and were concerned I would have to wait for them.

God intervenes in our situations when we commit them to Him.

Commit to the Lord your children, your marriage, your personal relationships and especially anything you may be tempted to be concerned about: *Casting the whole of your care [all your anxieties, all your worries, all your concerns, once and for all] on Him, for He cares for you affectionately and cares about you watchfully* (1 Peter 5:7).

In order to succeed at being ourselves, we must continually be committing ourselves to God, giving to Him those things that appear to be holding us back. Only God can take proper care of those types of situations.

In my own life I found that the more I tried to take care of things myself, the bigger mess my life became. I was quite independent and found it difficult to humble myself and admit that I needed help. However, when I finally submitted to God in these areas and found the joy of casting all my care on Him, I could not believe I had lived so long under such huge amounts of pressure.

Worry releases pressure; prayer releases peace.

You and I may find that we have a timetable for things to occur in our lives, and we may also find that things don't happen according to our timetable. It may be disappointing initially, but the best thing to do is *give it to God in prayer.* As we often say, *"Let go and let God."*

There is much to be done in our lives before we reach the fullness of our destiny.

When I look back over the years of my life, all I can say is, "Wow!" So much has happened that it is almost unbelievable.

Only God really knows what needs to be done, and He is the *only* One Who is qualified to do it. The more we sincerely commit ourselves to Him, the more progress we make.

Pray the prayer of commitment often. Remember, anytime, anywhere is an acceptable time for prayer.

THE PRAYER OF CONSECRATION

The final type of prayer is the prayer of consecration, the prayer in which we give ourselves to God. In the prayer of consecration, we dedicate our lives and all that we are to Him.

I recall sitting in a church service many years ago. It was missions Sunday, and as the organ played and we sang a song based on Isaiah, I was moved in my heart to offer myself to God for His service. I remember singing the words everyone else was singing, "Here I am, Lord..." "Send me!"

I had sung these same words on other mission Sundays, but this time it was different. Something was stirring in my heart and emotions. There were tears in my eyes, and I could feel that I was truly giving myself to God for His will to be accomplished in me.

I often think of that Sunday. Nothing happened right away; as a matter of fact, I don't recall anything particular happening for years after that. But somehow I know in my heart that my commitment to God that particular Sunday had something to do with the call I received into the ministry some years later.

In order for God to use us, we must consecrate ourselves to Him.

I still consecrate myself to God in prayer on a regular basis. I say, "Here I am, Lord. I am Yours; do with me as You please." Then sometimes I add, "I hope I like what You choose, Lord, but if I don't, do it anyway; Your will be done and not mine."

When we truly consecrate ourselves to the Lord, we lose the burden of trying to run our own lives. I would rather voluntarily follow God than struggle to get Him to follow me. He knows where He is going, and I know I will reach my destination safely if I allow Him to lead.

When we dedicate our children to the Lord, we are, in effect, giving them to Him for His purposes. We are saying, "Lord, I know You have a specific purpose for these children, and I want You to have Your way in their lives. I will raise them for You, not for myself, for Your purpose and will, not for my own."

Consecration is a powerful thing, but it must be sincere. It is quite easy to sing along with everyone else a song like "I Surrender All." We may even feel moved emotionally, but the real test is found in daily life when things don't always go the way we thought they would. Then we must sing again, "I Surrender All," consecrating ourselves to God afresh.

Consecration and/or dedication to God is the most important aspect of succeeding at being ourselves. We don't even know what we are supposed to be, let alone know how to become whatever it is. But as we regularly keep our lives on the altar in consecration to God, He will do the work that needs to be done in us, so He may do the work He desires to do *through* us.

Remember, all of these types of prayer are simple, and we don't need to complicate them. They can be used with ease whenever needed in life. We must never forget to do what we are told in God's Word: *Pray at all times (on every occasion, in every season) in the Spirit, with all [manner of] prayer and entreaty. To that end keep alert and watch with strong purpose and perseverance, interceding in behalf of all the saints (God's consecrated people)* (Ephesians 6:18).

SHORT AND SIMPLE IS MORE POWERFUL THAN LONG AND COMPLICATED

> *"And when you pray, do not keep on babbling like pagans, for they think they will be heard because of their many words. Do not be like them, for your Father knows what you need before you ask him."*
> *Matthew 6:7,8 NIV*

I believe God has instructed me to pray and make my requests with as few words as possible. As I follow this practice, I understand more and more why He told me to do so. I find if I can keep my request very simple and not confuse the issue by trying to come up with too many words, my prayer actually seems to be more clear and powerful.

We need to spend our energy releasing our faith, not repeating phrases over and over that only serve to make the prayer long and involved.

It amazes me that we as human beings are so deceived regarding the true value of things. We always think more is better, when actually nothing could be further from the truth. Sometimes the more we have, the less we appreciate it. The more things we have to take care of, the less we take proper care of anything. Oftentimes, more only brings confusion.

Sometimes I get confused about what I want to wear on a given day or to a certain event. I have pastor friends in India who don't experience this kind of confusion. When they go to their closet, they only have one suit, so they just put it on and go.

I am certainly not against being prosperous, nor am I against having a lot of clothes. Clothes are actually one of the material things in this life I really enjoy, and God has blessed me with an abundance of them. But I am using them as an example to make my point.

Unless we use wisdom and make a conscious effort to keep life simple, all of our abundance will only serve to bring confusion and unhappiness rather than peace and joy.

It has actually been difficult for me to keep my prayers short and simple. I don't mean that I am advocating praying only for a short period of time, but I am suggesting that each prayer be simple, direct, to the point and filled with faith. Let me give you an example.

If I need forgiveness, I can pray: "Lord, I lost my temper, and I'm sorry, I ask You to forgive me. I receive Your forgiveness, and I thank You for it, in Jesus' name. Amen!"

Or I can pray: "Oh, Lord, I'm so wretched. I feel so miserable. It seems that I just cannot do anything right. No matter how hard I try, I am always fouling up and making mistakes. I lost my temper, and now everyone is mad at me. I have made a fool of myself, and I just don't know what I'm going to do. I have got to stop getting mad.

"I'm so sorry, Father. Please forgive me. Oh, God, please forgive me. Please, Lord, I promise I will never do it again. Oh, Lord, I feel so guilty. I feel so bad. I am so ashamed of myself. I don't see how You can use me, God. I have so many problems.

"Well, Lord, I don't feel any better, but I will try to believe that I am forgiven."

I think you will agree that the first prayer would be much more powerful than the second.

Here's another example, a prayer for progress:

"Lord, I am weary of waiting to see progress in my life. I need for You either to do something that will bring a breakthrough in my circumstances or to give me a fresh anointing to wait. I trust You, Lord, to answer my prayer, and I want You to know that whatever Your answer may be, I love You."

Compare that version with this one:

"Lord, I just feel that I can't wait any longer to see a breakthrough. I have got to see something this week, God, or I don't think I can hold on any longer. I hear about everyone else's progress, and I feel that I don't ever make any progress. It has been so long, Father, since I have received any kind of blessing, and I am tired. I am weary. I am depressed. I am discouraged. I am disappointed. I feel like giving up..."

(I might stop at this point in the prayer and cry for a long time, then resume praying.)

"...God, I hope You are hearing me, because I seriously don't think I can go on one more day like this. I don't know what I'm doing wrong. Don't You love me anymore?

"Where are You, Lord? I can't feel Your Presence. I don't see You moving in my life. I don't know if I am hearing from You or not. I am confused. I feel worse now than when I started praying. What's wrong with me? I don't even know if I know how to pray. Oh, won't You please help me, Father?"

You can think of more examples on your own, but I hope these get my point across.

I began to realize that my problem in praying was that I didn't have faith that my prayer would get through if it was short, simple and to the point. I had fallen into the same trap that many people do — "the-longer-the-better" mentality. However, after praying, most of the time I felt confused and unsure, as though I still had not gotten the job done.

Now as I follow God's direction to keep it simple and make my request with the least amount of words possible, I experience a much greater release of my faith, and I know that God has heard me and will answer.

As I said previously, confidence in prayer is vital to success in any area. Be really honest with yourself about your prayer life and make adjustments wherever they are needed. If you are not praying enough, pray more. If your prayers are complicated, simplify them. If you need to keep them more of a secret just between you and God, then quit talking about them to everyone you meet.

The great thing about being convicted of error in our lives is that we can then make a change.

How Many Times Should We Pray About the Same Thing?

> *Keep on asking and it will be given you; keep on seeking and*
> *you will find; keep on knocking [reverently] and [the door]*
> *will be opened to you.*
> *For everyone who keeps on asking receives; and he who keeps*
> *on seeking finds; and to him who keeps on knocking, [the*
> *door] will be opened.*
> *Matthew 7:7,8*

It is difficult to lay down any strict rules on the subject of how often to pray about the same thing. I have heard some people say, "Pray repeatedly until you see the breakthrough." I have heard others say, "If you pray more than once for something, then you don't believe you got it the first time."

I don't believe we can make any strict rules, but I do think there are some guidelines that may apply to help us have even more confidence in our prayer power.

If my children told me their shoes were worn out and asked me to get them some new ones, I would probably respond, "OK, I'll get them as soon as I can."

What I would want from my children is trust. I would want them to trust me to do what they asked me to do. I wouldn't mind, and might even like it, if they occasionally said, "Boy, Mom, I'm sure looking forward to those new shoes," or "I'm excited about my new shoes, Mom; I'll be glad when I get them and can wear them." Both of those statements would declare to me that they believed I was going to do what I promised. They would actually be reminding me of my promise, but in a way that would not question my integrity.

On the other hand, if they came back to me an hour later and made the same request again, it might irritate me. If they said, "Mom, my shoes are worn out, and I'm asking you to get me some new ones," I would think, "I heard you the first time, and I told you I would get them as soon as I can. What is your problem?"

I believe sometimes when we ask God the same thing over and over, it is a sign of doubt and unbelief, not of faith and persistence.

When I ask the Lord for something in prayer, and that thing comes to my mind or heart again later, I talk to Him about it again. But when I do, I refrain from asking Him the same thing as if I think He didn't hear me the first time.

When I pray, I thank the Lord that He is working on the situation I prayed about previously. But I don't come back and repray the same thing all over again.

Faithful, persistent prayer builds even more faith and confidence in us as we continue to pray. The stronger our confidence is, the better off we are.

Therefore, I urge you to do things that build confidence, not things that tear it down. Do things that honor God, not things that dishonor Him.

In Matthew 7, Jesus tells us to ask and to keep on asking, and we will receive. He also tells us to knock and keep on knocking, and it will be opened to us, to seek and keep on seeking, and we will find.

As I have stated, I believe this message refers to persistence not repetition. We should keep pressing on and never give up — if we are sure we are pursuing something that is the will of God. It is definitely the will of God for each of us to succeed at being ourselves and find fulfillment in being all He designed us to be. Therefore, I believe that faithful persistent prayer is an important factor in reaching that goal.

BE A BELIEVER, NOT A BEGGAR

> Let us then fearlessly and confidently and boldly draw near to
> the throne of grace (the throne of God's unmerited favor to us
> sinners), that we may receive mercy [for our failures] and find
> grace to help in good time for every need [appropriate help
> and well-timed help, coming just when we need it].
> Hebrews 4:16

When you and I pray, we need to make sure we approach God as believers, not as beggars. Remember, according to Hebrews 4:16, we are to come boldly to the throne: not beggarly, but boldly; not belligerently, but boldly.

Be sure to keep the balance. Stay respectful, but be bold. Approach God with confidence. Believe He delights in your prayers and is ready to answer any request that is in accordance with His will.

As believers, we should know the Word of God, which is His will; therefore, it should be easy for us to pray according to God's will. Don't approach God wondering if what you are asking is His will. Settle that issue in your heart *before* you pray.

There are times when I really don't know what God's will is in a certain situation, and I tell Him so when I pray. In those cases, I simply ask for His will to be done.

In either case, we should pray with boldness and confidence.

BELIEVE GOD HEARS YOU!

> *And this is the confidence (the assurance, the privilege of boldness) which we have in Him: [we are sure] that if we ask anything (make any request) according to His will (in agreement with His own plan), He listens to and hears us.*
> *And if (since) we [positively] know that He listens to us in whatever we ask, we also know [with settled and absolute knowledge] that we have [granted us as our present possessions] the requests made of Him.*
> *1 John 5:14,15*

When you pray, believe God hears you!

In John 11:41,42 just before He called Lazarus forth from the tomb, Jesus prayed:

> *...Father, I thank You that You have heard Me.*
> *Yes, I know You always hear and listen to Me, but I have said this on account of and for the benefit of the people standing around, so that they may believe that You did send Me [that You have made Me Your Messenger].*

What confidence! To the Pharisees that must have seemed like a haughty spirit. Their response must have been, "Who does He think He is?"

Just as Satan did not want Jesus to have that kind of confidence, he does not want us to have that kind of confidence either. But I am encouraging you one more time before ending this book:

Be confident!

Make a decision that you are a believer, not a beggar. Go to the throne in Jesus' name — His name will get attention!

I am not even famous like Jesus is, but people like to use my name. My employees like to say, "I work for Joyce Meyer," my friends like to say, "I know Joyce Meyer," and my children like to say, "Joyce Meyer is my mother." They especially like to do that when they want favor with someone, and they think those they are approaching may give them more favor if they mention my name.

If that works for us as human beings, just think how well it must work in the heavenly realm — especially when we use the name that is above all other names — the blessed name of Jesus! (Philippians 2:9-11.)

Go boldly. Go in the name of Jesus. Go with confidence, and go determined to succeed at being yourself.

CONCLUSION

CONCLUSION

To summarize the most important point of this entire book, let me say in closing: *you will never sense fulfillment in life unless you reach the goal of being yourself.*

Jesus died so that you could be free from comparing yourself with others and free from living in the agony of trying to copy them.

And may the God of peace Himself sanctify you through and through [separate you from profane things, make you pure and wholly consecrated to God]; and may your spirit and soul and body be preserved sound and complete [and found] blameless at the coming of our Lord Jesus Christ (the Messiah).
1 THESSALONIANS 5:23

In his book entitled *Sanctification,* Charles Finney wrote: "...sanctification cannot be attained by attempting to copy the experience of others. It is very common for convicted sinners, or for Christians inquiring after entire sanctification, in their blindness, to ask others to relate their experience, to mark minutely the detail of all their exercises, and then set themselves to pray for, and make direct efforts to attain the same class of exercises, not seeming to understand that they can no more exercise feelings in detail like others than they can look like others.

"Human experiences differ as human countenances differ. The whole history of a man's former state of mind comes in of course to modify his present and future experience; so that the precise train of feelings which may be requisite in your case, and which will actually occur if you are ever sanctified, will not in all its details coincide with the exercises of any other human being. It is of vast importance for you to understand that you can be no copyist in any true religious experience; and that you are in great danger of being deceived by Satan whenever you attempt to copy the experience of others. I beseech you therefore to cease from praying for, or trying to obtain, the precise experience of any person whatever."[1]

Charles Finney lived and ministered in the 1800s. As I teach the Word of God almost 150 years after him, I find it encouraging that the message is still the same.

Sanctification, of course, is the state of perfect holiness and is reached in degrees through the work of the Holy Spirit in our lives.

Vine's Complete Expository Dictionary of Old and New Testament Words states that *sanctification* is "separation to God....the separation of the believer from evil things and ways. This sanctification is God's will for the believer...and His purpose in calling him by the gospel...it must be learned from God...as He teaches it by His Word...and it must be pursued by the believer, earnestly and undeviatingly....For the holy character...is not vicarious, i.e., it cannot be transferred or imputed, it is an individual possession, built up, little by little, as the result of obedience to the Word of God, and of following the example of Christ...in the power of the Holy Spirit."[2]

We are not sanctified by following any other person, but only as we follow Christ as our example. Part of this sanctification or perfection must certainly be the accomplishment of fulfilling our individual destinies, for how can we be sanctified if we are out of the will of God for our lives, or found cringing in fear, doubt, self-rejection and unbelief?

Charles Finney states that sanctification cannot come by means of copying any other person. I agree and also say that none of us will succeed at being ourselves, none of us will be free and able to enjoy our life, by copying any other individual.

My intention when I embarked upon this project, which has required several hundred hours of my time in its preparation, was to help you succeed in being yourself. I believe that to the best of my ability I have completed my goal.

May God richly bless you as you press on toward the high call of being all you can be in, through, by and for Christ Jesus.

PRAYER FOR A PERSONAL
RELATIONSHIP WITH THE LORD

God wants you to receive His free gift of salvation. Jesus wants to save you and fill you with the Holy Spirit more than anything. If you have never invited Jesus, the Prince of Peace, to be your Lord and Savior, I invite you to do so now. Pray the following prayer, and if you are really sincere about it, you will experience a new life in Christ.

Father,

You loved the world so much, You gave Your only begotten Son to die for our sins so that whoever believes in Him will not perish, but have eternal life.

Your Word says we are saved by grace through faith as a gift from You. There is nothing we can do to earn salvation.

I believe and confess with my mouth that Jesus Christ is Your Son, the Savior of the world. I believe He died on the cross for me and bore all of my sins, paying the price for them. I believe in my heart that You raised Jesus from the dead.

I ask You to forgive my sins. I confess Jesus as my Lord. According to Your Word, I am saved and will spend eternity with You! Thank You, Father. I am so grateful! In Jesus' name, amen.

See John 3:16; Ephesians 2:8,9; Romans 10:9,10; 1 Corinthians 15:3,4; 1 John 1:9; 4:14-16; 5:1,12,13.

ENDNOTES

Introduction

[1] God will restore our soul. David said in Psalm 23:1,3: *The LORD is my shepherd.... He restoreth my soul...* (KJV). We see from reading Luke 4:18 that Jesus was sent to bring restoration to our lives. *The Spirit of the Lord is upon me* [Jesus], *because he hath anointed me to preach the gospel to the poor; he hath sent me to heal the brokenhearted, to preach deliverance to the captives, and recovering of sight to the blind, to set at liberty them that are bruised* (KJV).

Chapter 1

[1] *Webster's II New College Dictionary* (Boston/New York: Houghton Mifflin Company, 1995), s.v. "accept."

[2] Webster's II, s.v. "acceptance."

Chapter 2

[1] Based on a definition from James Strong, "Hebrew and Chaldee Dictionary" in *Strong's Exhaustive Concordance of the Bible* (Nashville: Abingdon, 1890), p. 58, entry #3810, s.v. "Lo-debar," 2 Samuel 9:4 — *"pastureless."*

Chapter 6

[1] *American Dictionary of the English Language,* 10th Ed. (San Francisco: Foundation for American Christian Education, 1998). Facsimile of Noah Webster's 1828 edition, permission to reprint by G. & C. Merriam Company, copyright 1967 & 1995 (Renewal) by Rosalie J. Slater, s.v. "POSSIBLE."

[2] Webster's 1828 edition, s.v. "POSSIBILITY."

[3] *Houston Chronicle:* Knight-Ridder Tribune News, "After 100 years, things are jelling nicely," 4 March 1997, p. 1C; David Lyman, Knight-Ridder Tribune News, "Colorful dessert marks first century/100 years of Jell-O," 16 April 1997, p. 1F, reprinted with permission of Knight Ridder/Tribune Information Services; Associated Press, "Family got little dough in gramps' Jell-O sale in '99," 18 May 1997, p. 2D; as reported in *In Other Words...* (6130 Barrington, Beaumont, Texas 77706), *The Christian Communicator's Research Service* 7, no. 3, "Patience."

[4] (Tulsa: Harrison House, 1995), p. 227.

[5] W.E. Vine, *Vine's Complete Expository Dictionary of Old and New Testament Words* (Nashville: Thomas Nelson Inc., 1984), "An Expository Dictionary of New Testament Words," p. 462, s.v. "PATIENCE, PATIENT, PATIENTLY," **A. Nouns,** HUPOMONE.

Chapter 8

[1] Strong, "Greek Dictionary of the New Testament," p. 77, entry #5485, s.v. "favor" and "grace."

[2] Webster's 1828 edition, s.v. "mercy."

Chapter 9

[1] Paragraph is from *Enjoying Where You Are on the Way to Where You Are Going* (Tulsa: Harrison House, 1996), p. 40.

Chapter 10

[1] Vine, p. 468, s.v. "PERSECUTE, PERSECUTION," **A. Verbs.**, DIOKO.

[2] A talent was a very large standard of measure. "A talent seems to have been a full weight for an able man to carry (2 Kings 5:23)." Merrill F. Unger, *The New Unger's Bible Dictionary*, Ed. R.K. Harrison, (Chicago: Moody Press, 1988), p. 844, s.v. "Talent."

Chapter 11

[1] Strong, "Greek Dictionary," p. 40, entry #2631, s.v. "condemnation," Romans 8:1.

[2] Vine, p. 119, s.v. "CONDEMN, CONDEMNATION," **B. Nouns.**, KRIMA.

[3] Strong, "Greek Dictionary," p. 39, entry #2607, s.v. "condemn," 3 John 3:20,21.

[4] Strong, "Greek Dictionary," p. 40, entry #2632, s.v. "condemn," Matthew 12:41.

[5] Strong, "Greek Dictionary," p. 40, entry #2613, s.v. "condemn," Luke 6:37.

[6] Strong, "Greek Dictionary," p. 43, entry #2919, s.v. "condemn," John 3:17.

[7] Vine, pp. 229, 230, s.v. "FEAR, FEARFUL, FEARFULNESS," **A. Nouns.**, 1. PHOBOS.

Conclusion

[1] Charles Finney, *Sanctification* (Fort Washington, Pennsylvania: Christian Literature Crusade, 1994 printing), p. 15.

[2] Vine, pp. 545, 546, s.v. "SANCTIFICATION, SANCTIFY," **A. Noun.**, HAGIASMOS.

REFERENCES

BIBLE TRANSLATIONS ────────────────────────────

Some Scripture quotations are taken from *The Heart of Paul: Biblical Truth in Today's Language* by Ben Campbell Johnson. Copyright © 1976 by Ben Campbell Johnson, published by A Great Love, Inc., Toccoa, Georgia 30577. Used by permission.

Scripture quotations marked (NIV) are taken from the *Holy Bible, New International Version®*. NIV®. Copyright © 1973, 1978, 1984 by International Bible Society. Used by permission of Zondervan Publishing.

Verses marked (TLB) are taken from *The Living Bible* © 1971. Used by permission of Tyndale House Publishers, Inc., Wheaton, Illinois 60189. All rights reserved.

Scripture quotations marked MESSAGE are taken from *The Message: New Testament With Psalms and Proverbs* by Eugene H. Peterson. Copyright © 1993, 1994, 1995 by Eugene H. Peterson, NavPress, P. O. Box 35001, Colorado Springs, Colorado 80935. Used with permission.

Scripture quotations marked MOFFATT are taken from *The Bible. A New Translation*. Copyright © 1950, 1952, 1953, 1954 by James A.R. Moffatt, Harper & Row Publishers, Inc., New York, New York.

Scripture quotations marked (NKJV) are taken from *The New King James Version*. Copyright © 1979, 1980, 1982, Thomas Nelson, Inc. Used by permission. All rights reserved.

Scripture quotations marked PHILLIPS are taken from the *New Testament in Modern English*, (Rev. Ed.) by J.B. Phillips. Copyright © 1958, 1960, 1972 by J.B. Phillips. Reprinted by permission of Macmillan Publishing Co., New York, New York.

Scripture quotations marked WEYMOUTH are taken from *Weymouth's New Testament in Modern Speech* by Richard Francis Weymouth. Copyright © 1978 by Kregel Publications, a division of Kregel Inc. Harper & Row Publishers, Inc., New York, New York.

BIBLE REFERENCES ────────────────────────────

Strong, James. *Strong's Exhaustive Concordance of the Bible*. Nashville: Abingdon Press, 1890.

Unger, Merrill F. *The New Unger's Bible Dictionary,* Ed. R.K. Harrison. Chicago: Moody Press, 1988.

Vine, W.E. *Vine's Complete Expository Dictionary of Old and New Testament Words.* Nashville: Thomas Nelson Inc., 1984.

DICTIONARIES

American Dictionary of the English Language, 10th Ed. (San Francisco: Foundation for American Christian Education, 1998). Facsimile of Noah Webster's 1828 edition, permission to reprint by G. & C. Merriam Company, copyright 1967 & 1995 (Renewal) by Rosalie J. Slater.

Webster's II New College Dictionary. Boston/New York: Houghton Mifflin Company, 1995.

ABOUT THE AUTHOR

JOYCE MEYER is one of the world's leading practical Bible teachers. A #1 *New York Times* bestselling author, she has written more than seventy inspirational books, including *The Confident Woman, I Dare You*, the entire Battlefield of the Mind family of books, her first venture into fiction with *The Penny*, and many others. She has also released thousands of audio teachings as well as a complete video library. Joyce's *Enjoying Everyday Life*® radio and television programs are broadcast around the world, and she travels extensively conducting conferences. Joyce and her husband, Dave, are the parents of four grown children and make their home in St. Louis, Missouri.

TO CONTACT THE AUTHOR,
PLEASE WRITE:

Joyce Meyer Ministries
P.O. Box 655
Fenton, MO 63026
USA
(636) 349-0303
www.joycemeyer.org

Joyce Meyer Ministries—Canada
Lambeth Box 1300
London, ON N6P 1T5
Canada
1-800-727-9673

Joyce Meyer Ministries—Australia
Locked Bag 77
Mansfield Delivery Centre
Queensland 4122
Australia
(07) 3349 1200

Joyce Meyer Ministries—England
P.O. Box 1549
Windsor SL4 1GT
United Kingdom
01753 831102

Joyce Meyer Ministries—South Africa
P.O. Box 5
Cape Town 8000
South Africa
(27) 21-701-1056

OTHER BOOKS BY JOYCE MEYER

New Day, New You Devotional

I Dare You

The Penny

The Power of Simple Prayer

The Everyday Life Bible

The Confident Woman

Look Great, Feel Great

*Battlefield of the Mind**

Battlefield of the Mind Devotional

Battlefield of the Mind for Teens

Battlefield of the Mind for Kids

Approval Addiction

Ending Your Day Right

21 Ways to Finding Peace and Happiness

The Secret Power of Speaking God's Word

Seven Things That Steal Your Joy

Starting Your Day Right

Beauty for Ashes (revised edition)

*How to Hear from God**

Knowing God Intimately

The Power of Forgiveness

*Study Guide available for this title.

The Power of Determination

The Power of Being Positive

The Secrets of Spiritual Power

The Battle Belongs to the Lord

The Secrets to Exceptional Living

Eight Ways to Keep the Devil Under Your Feet

Teenagers Are People Too!

Filled with the Spirit

Celebration of Simplicity

The Joy of Believing Prayer

Never Lose Heart

Being the Person God Made You to Be

A Leader in the Making

"Good Morning, This Is God!" (gift book)

Jesus—Name Above All Names

Making Marriage Work
(previously published as *Help Me—I'm Married!*)

Reduce Me to Love

Be Healed in Jesus' Name

How to Succeed at Being Yourself

Weary Warriors, Fainting Saints

Be Anxious for Nothing *

Straight Talk Omnibus

Don't Dread

Managing Your Emotions

Healing the Brokenhearted

Me and My Big Mouth! *

Prepare to Prosper

Do It Afraid!

Expect a Move of God in Your Life . . . Suddenly!

Enjoying Where You Are on the Way to Where You Are Going

A New Way of Living

When, God, When?

Why, God, Why?

The Word, the Name, the Blood

Tell Them I Love Them

Peace

If Not for the Grace of God *

JOYCE MEYER SPANISH TITLES

Las Siete Cosas Que Te Roban el Gozo
(Seven Things That Steal Your Joy)

Empezando Tu Dia Bien (Starting Your Day Right)

BOOKS BY DAVE MEYER

Life Lines